# Relax! It's Only Social Media

# Relax! It's Only Social Media

## A NO-NONSENSE GUIDE TO SOCIAL NETWORKING FOR YOU AND YOUR BUSINESS

## Luan Wise

luanwise.co.uk

Graphic design by Neil Simpson, the-brightside.co.uk
Illustration by Phil Clarke, clarketoons.com

Copyright acknowledgements
- Aimia for permission to reference 'Staring at the Sun: Identifying, understanding and influencing social media users'
- eMarketer.com for permission to use internet user statistics
- John Atkinson, wronghands1.com for permission to use 'vintage social networking'
- Simon Sinek Inc., startwithwhy.com for permission to share the Start with Why message.
- Tom Fishburne, marketoonist.com for permission to use 'voice of the brand', 'the big idea' and 'target market'
- Jan Kietzmann for permission to reproduce the 'honeycomb of social media', copyright Kelley School of Business, Indiana University

ISBN-13: 9781535557290
ISBN-10: 153555729X

**Praise for**
**Relax! It's Only Social Media**

A clear and thorough guide to social media marketing for business stakeholders.
Andy Fernandez
Bookshop and Library Manager, The Chartered Institute of Marketing

• • •

Perfectly pitched. Luan's guide will be invaluable for anyone who wants a no-nonsense approach to social media, even the most reluctant.
Alex Butler
Digital Transformation Leader, Kindred HQ Founder

• • •

This is a fantastic resource and a 'must read' for anyone who engages with social media; whether you are an experienced professional or cutting your teeth in the business world. Luan gives you insights about strategy and how it underpins the practicalities of engaging an audience; making social media platforms work for your business objectives. This book is peppered with practical advice and leads you through the issues and challenges associated with our digital world. Luan not only demystifies social media, but will also give experienced professionals food for thought. Alongside her strategic insight, Luan also highlights the importance of business relationships with customers, the art of how to listen to customers and the importance of measurement. It doesn't stop there! Luan also gives excellent advice about how to utilise social media for your career and will challenge you to think about how you market yourself as a professional.
Dr Laura M. Chamberlain
Lecturer in Consumer Behaviour, Customer Experience and Marketing, Aston Business School

• • •

# Contents

# About the author

Luan Wise is a chartered marketer with more than 15 years' experience of working with clients including Hilton, Royal Mail, Panasonic, and the University of Cambridge.

Luan's career in marketing started 'web first', managing content and building online communities. She helped many businesses to produce their first websites. For most of her agency-side career, Luan worked for Hilton, planning and managing complex multimedia, multi-site promotional campaigns for its national and international chain of health clubs. In 2007 Luan switched to become a client-side marketer, joining a new business operating in the newly liberalised postal marketplace. With Luan's support, the business's annual sales rocketed from £3 million to £60 million over the next five years.

In 2009 Luan discovered social media, and hasn't put a smartphone down since.

Her practical marketing expertise has awarded Luan many invitations to speak at business events. She's also won many accolades, including being named one of the top five female marketers by LinkedIn UK for its International Women's Day campaign, and being included in the South West's '42 under 42' list of the region's brightest talents. Luan is an active ambassador for the Chartered Institute of Marketing and the Direct Marketing Association.

Today, Luan runs a successful marketing consultancy, providing marketing advice, practical hands-on support, and training. Luan is known for her enthusiasm. Her audiences also refer to her as 'inspiring': she makes things happen and gets results.

When not working with a client on the sustainable growth of their business, Luan can be found with her head in a book, a coffee in hand, or buying more shoes she really doesn't need.

# Introduction

You can dive into social media head-first and see what happens, or you can take the time to research, evaluate, plan and execute your approach. I choose the second option.

It's easy to get carried away and blindly create profiles on new social media platforms, regardless of whether your target audience is even present. With a smartphone in your pocket, it's easy to post content and release it to the world. But, what's the point?

There are lots of 'how to' books on social media, and no end of blogs, but there are few that address the fear that many people have about using social media – the fear of not really knowing what to do, and not wanting to get it wrong.

My aim, in writing this book, is to bring the business of social media back to basics: to compare the new with the traditional, to adopt a planned approach, and to ensure that you know how you can get results for your business.

## Who is this book for?

If you're a marketer or a business owner, director, manager with responsibility for marketing, this book is for you. If you're involved in customer service, recruitment or sales you will also find this helpful to your day-to-day role. You'll probably be using social media already, but know you could be using it better.

## What you will learn in this book

- That social media is not just about technology
- That everything needs to start with *why*
- What is the point of social media
- Which social media platform/s you should be using
- That social media is *not* a strategy
- How to get ready to do business on social media
- Why you need to listen first, then engage
- That marketing is all about telling stories to the right people, at the right point in the buying process
- That the power of content lies in its potential to start a conversation
- If you know what you're looking for, you can focus on the measurements that matter.

Wherever the future lies with social media, it's only one channel of communication. So relax!

The only thing we can be certain of with social media is that it will change, so let's embrace change and focus on knowing where we want to be, and on developing a plan that will help get us there.

## Using this book

This book is a step-by-step guide through the social media planning process. The chapter summaries below will help you see the journey we're going to take. At the end of the book you will find some useful resources, which include tools and links to further reading, e-learning courses and other downloads.

## Chapter 1 The business of social networking

Frightened of social media? There's no need. It's nothing new! The book begins by looking at a brief history of social media, the evolution of marketing and the business of building relationships. When people know, like and trust you, they will do business with you. Social media is a supporting tool.

## Chapter 2 What's the point of social media?

In this chapter we take the first steps towards understanding how to make social media work for you and your business. We start with *why*. We learn about the different types of social media user, the functional building blocks that help us make sense of social media, and the different platforms available. Most importantly, we identify that social media is *not* a strategy.

## Chapter 3 Making a good first impression

The web is your Hollywood agent, speaking for you whenever you are not around. It's so important to make a good first impression, but all too often profiles are set up quickly and never revisited. This chapter contains advice on how to get it right, so you're ready to do business.

## Chapter 4 Finding your audience on social media

Having a profile and posting some content on social media will not naturally create an audience; you've got to go out and find your audience. You also need to know who you want to be in that audience. You've got to make connections and become known.

## Chapter 5 Mastering the art of listening

Listening gives you the opportunity to gain a business advantage. Insight into what your customers, competitors and peers are thinking, saying and doing can provide valuable direction to marketing, product development, customer service and recruitment activities. The ultimate aim of social media listening is to discover all the content relevant to an organisation, brand or issue in a timely fashion. In this chapter, you learn how to master the art of listening.

## Chapter 6 Content marketing and storytelling

The era of mass marketing has gone. We used to shout loudly and repeatedly at people to get attention. We used to send out large-volume direct marketing campaigns to as many people as possible, hoping that a small percentage would respond. Thankfully, advertisers have now learnt that less is more, and a considered use of data and targeting can leverage the same, if not better, results. Good marketers have focused their efforts on being in the right place, at the right time, with the right message. It's all about content: words, knowledge and information.

## Chapter 7  Measurements that matter

Q: What makes a metric meaningful?

A: When you see the metric, do you know what you need to do?

If the answer is 'no', you're probably looking at a vanity metric. The answer needs to be 'yes'! This chapter addresses the mistake of looking at meaningless metrics, and shows you how to focus on the measurements that really matter to you and your business.

## Chapter 8  Making it happen

Individuals and businesses that are successful with social media don't fall into the 'social media's the answer; what's the question?' trap. They define what they are trying to achieve, and the best way to achieve it, then find the tools they need to achieve their goals.

# CHAPTER 1

## The business of social networking

Frightened of social media? There's no need. It's nothing new! The book begins by looking at a brief history of social media, the evolution of marketing and the business of building relationships. When people know, like and trust you, they will do business with you. Social media is a supporting tool.

How often do you sit and think 'I need to post something on my Facebook page', or 'I need to do something on LinkedIn'?

How does it make you feel?

Do you (a) look at your to-do list and try to find something (anything) else to do instead, (b) sigh and post the first thing that comes into your head, or (c) take a quick look at your marketing plan and check off the next piece of content?

Since you're reading this book, I'm guessing your answer is (a) or (b) …

As a seasoned user of social media platforms, it's sometimes easy for me to forget what it's like to be a beginner in using social media. I don't believe I experienced any fears when I set up my LinkedIn account in January 2008 or my Twitter profile in March 2009. Once I took the decision to look at what social media was all about (OK, I took a little bit of convincing by a very early adopter), I simply wanted to explore what these new tools could do for me and the business I was working for. I wasn't on social media because it was the 'done thing' – I was there to explore new opportunities.

Eight years later, it feels like social media has become over-complicated. It's become misunderstood and surrounded in mystery and the dark arts – just like SEO (search engine optimisation). A plethora of social media experts have emerged to show individuals and companies *how* to use the various platforms. But knowing *how* to use them isn't the same as understanding *why* you should use them.

There's something about social media that makes some people (perhaps you?) bury their head in the sand and pretend it's just not happening. Others may feel fear and anxiety.

I believe these fears are not unique to social media. People have always been afraid of the unknown (and change). All businesses fear bad

*There are too many options. I don't know where to start or what to do.*

*I'm afraid I'll say something bad. Or someone else will say something bad. I don't want to open myself or my business up to negativity.*

*If I use social media, people will try to poach my clients or my employees.*

publicity, losing business and employees, don't they? There's also the barrier of lack of time and resource. Again, these factors are not unique to social media. While some people do appear to be documenting their entire lives online, it's not necessary to do so.

I have discovered that people who have not had the opportunity to explore social media are somewhat fearful of 'joining in', particularly within a business context. There's a fear of simply not knowing enough, and therefore people hold back. Even people who have had social media profiles for a while have told me about their fears of not being able to use social media intelligently, relevantly and sustainably, and have said they don't know where to turn to get the answers.

This book aims to address these fears and guide you through some of the platforms available, the various uses of social media, how to make a good first impression, how to find your audience, listen to what they need, and respond with relevant content. However, this book is not a 'how to' guide to social media – I have listed resources at the back of the book for that. I want to help you understand the planning process that will ensure you and your business get results, and I want to help you feel more confident and relaxed about your use of social media.

## Social media is not just about technology

Yes, social media is about technology – it enables information to spread more rapidly and more widely than ever – but if you strip away the technology from social media, we can see the activities we have always done.

John Atkinson of Wrong Hands puts social media into perspective in this cartoon:

Image used with permission of the artist.

LinkedIn has replaced the Rolodex and those nice books with plastic inserts for collecting business cards. We no longer send postcards when we're on holiday – we post on Facebook, uploading photos from our smartphones. Birthday and festive greetings are also taking place online, much to my disappointment; I remain a huge fan of sending cards via the postal service.

Technology has cleared our desks, and the mobile revolution has put power in our pockets. Today's smartphone has more power than the last generation's computers, and it allows us to do more things faster – but what we do is not really different, or new.

## Digital wisdom

In 2001, US author Mark Prensky invented the term 'digital native' to describe the post-millennial generation who would grow up in an online world. He said: 'Our students today are all "native speakers" of the digital language of computers, video games and the internet'.

The assumption that people who were 'born digital' have an inherent understanding of technology is obvious, but while they might understand what buttons to press (or where to swipe), that doesn't mean they're ready to use today's technology. Prensky notes 'it's very serious because the single biggest problem facing education today is that our digital immigrant instructors, who speak an outdated language (that of the pre-digital age) are struggling to teach a population that speaks an entirely new language.'

The classification of people into digital natives and digital immigrants is controversial, yet the situation it creates in the workplace remains. While social media is not a strategy in itself, its use does require a plan, and all too often digital natives are asked to carry out a firm's social media activity, but given no direction. Their lack of experience means they dive straight in without asking the right questions first. As Tom Fishburne illustrates, social media activity is all too often assigned to an intern,

*Image used with permission of the artist.*

who will not ask the rights questions about business strategy, and if senior staff do not understand social media they may not brief interns adequately.

I often come across business situations where digital natives are advising business owners that they 'must be on Facebook', simply because that's the social media platform *they* use to communicate with their friends and follow brands they like. Luckily, some business owners question this, and I have helped them to carry out research to identify which social media platforms and activities would be most effective for their business, their objectives and their customers. Employees and their friends are not necessarily your target audience. (Read more on target audiences in Chapter 4.) Traditional media have clear audience definitions with audited circulation figures, and planners can justify recommendations with data. Perhaps because social media is perceived to be 'free', traditional media planning is glossed over. Stakeholder opinions, including those of fellow employees, are important, but unless they truly represent your target audience, social media activities shouldn't be about what *they* like, or what they want to see – no business would survive if that's how marketing was planned!

## The evolution of marketing

Stories have been shared in every culture as a form of education and entertainment since symbols were first painted on cave walls. Stories have been told using music, dance and art as well as the spoken and written word. Storytelling is a way of sharing and interpreting experiences.

Just as we have progressed from cave paintings, marketing has moved on from simple exchanges of trade, to a period of mass production, to a time of pure sales orientation, and finally to the realisation that we need to have a marketing responsibility that focuses on the customer, not just the product. Over time the media channels we use to communicate, and build relationships in business, have also experienced a significant pace of change:

- Radio took 38 years to reach 50 million listeners.
- Television took 13 years to reach 50 million viewers.
- The internet only took 4 years to reach 50 million users.

Previously, marketers controlled their dialogue with consumers through television, radio, newspapers and magazines. Everything was broadcast. Now conversation is two-way, it's happening in real time, and it's as much user-generated as it is advertiser-generated.

Just as television changed media consumption from listening (radio) to watching, social media has created media producers. It is now possible for anyone to publish content, from anywhere, at any time – and it is also possible to consume content from anywhere, at any time.

# A brief history of social media

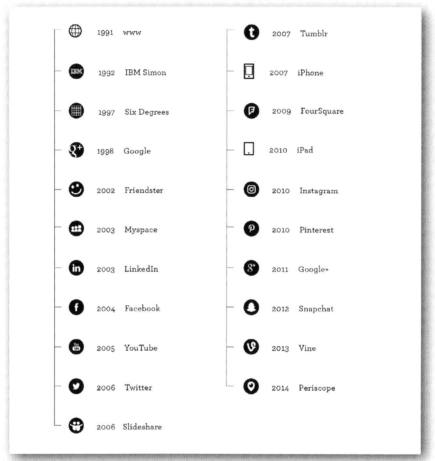

*Figure 1.1. Social media timeline.*

Social media has been evolving since Sir Tim Berners-Lee invented the World Wide Web in 1991. Figure 1.1 shows a timeline of events.

**Six Degrees**, launched in 1997, is considered to be the first social network (it closed in 2001). It enabled users to upload a profile and make friends with other users, but at this time the internet's infrastructure wasn't really ready for social networking and, while the site had millions of registered users, its growth was limited due to the low numbers of people connected to the internet.

By 2000, around 100 million people had access to the internet, and it became quite common for people to engage socially online.

**Friendster** was founded in 2002 (and closed in 2015), pioneering the online connection of real-world friends. **Myspace** (founded in 2003) was the largest social networking site from 2005–08, when **Facebook** overtook it. Before long there were dozens of other websites providing social media services. **Flickr** was one of the earliest photo-sharing sites. **Tumblr**, a microblogging website, started in 2007, and **Foursquare**, a location-based app, was also quite popular for a while (it was founded in 2009). From 2003, when **LinkedIn** was launched specifically for professionals, social media also became popular for businesses and marketers, who could see the opportunities it presented.

Fuelling the growth of social media is, of course, the smartphone. In 1992 IBM showcased the IBM Simon at the 1992 COMDEX (Computer Dealers' Exhibition): in doing so, they introduced the world to the first smartphone. It was the first time telephony features had been combined with the features of a personal computer. The term 'smartphone' was first introduced in 1995, the Blackberry gained mass popularity in 2006, but then Apple introduced the iPhone in 2007 – one of the first smartphones to use a multi-touch interface. Smartphones have become an important part of daily life, in terms of providing connectivity and efficient ways of working. I'd be lost without mine.

## What is social media?

I like Wikipedia's explanation: 'social media is an umbrella term that defines the various activities that integrate technology, social interaction and the construction of words, video and audio.'

There are hundreds of social media services, which take on many different forms, including:

- **social bookmarking**, such as StumbleUpon and Delicious: these services are publicly viewable lists of websites recommended by other users;
- **social news**, such as Digg and Reddit: these services are peer-based lists of recommended articles;
- **social geolocation**: services such as Foursquare and MeetUp bring people together in real life;
- **community-building** services provide the opportunity to comment and share information and content (for example, Wikipedia and TripAdvisor);
- **social content-sharing**, including blogs, video, images and audio (for example, Tumblr, Flickr and YouTube);
- **social networking** services, such as Facebook and LinkedIn: these have been developed to facilitate the exchange of information between groups of friends, family, colleagues and peers.

Social networking platforms have more specific functionality than other social media services, including personalised user profiles, the facility to post a status update (e.g. 'what's on your mind?'), groups for communities to hold discussions, and private messaging between users.

# Networking

> If people like you they'll listen to you, but if
> they trust you they'll do business with you.
> ZIG ZIGLAR

Business networking is all about making, and leveraging, connections to build relationships that can create or respond to business opportunities. Many business people (me included) believe that good networking is a more cost-effective way of building awareness, and generating new business, than paid-for advertising efforts.

But that doesn't mean it's quick, or easy. Good networking involves identifying the right places to network, finding the right people to network with, and nurturing mutually beneficial relationships. By its nature, networking involves building credibility and trust. When people know, like and trust you, they will do business with you.

Good networking is also about people being able to find you when they do an online search for the skills you offer, and having an effective online presence on the right social media platforms is the key to achieving this. Chapter 3 will look at how to make a good first impression on social media. Chapter 8 will review how to measure your success

Once you have made connections, you have the opportunity to become known among a wider network. Online networking lets you network 24/7, regardless of where you are in the world. Just as technology provides a new solution for the business card holder, we must not forget that social media provides support to real-life networking, allowing you to prepare for meetings, follow up meetings, and keep in touch with ease. There's no more letting people you haven't yet met in real life know that you'll be wearing a red carnation or carrying a newspaper – they can see what you look like on your LinkedIn profile! And with a status update or two a week, it's easy to stay in front of people with news of what you're working on. Through effective networking you can become the known and recommended expert, so that when a need arises you'll be at the front of their mind and they will consider you for the opportunity.

• • •

In this book we'll be looking in some detail at the 'big 5' platforms for social networking – LinkedIn, Twitter, Facebook, Instagram and Google+ – and how they can get results for you and your business. Let's find out a bit more about them …

## LinkedIn
LinkedIn started out in the living room of co-founder Reid Hoffman in 2002, and officially launched on 5 May 2003. Its mission is to 'connect the world's professionals to make them more productive and successful' and

its vision is to 'create economic opportunity for every professional'. As I write (June 2016), Microsoft has agreed to purchase LinkedIn for $26.2 billion. The companies share a common mission – empowering people and organisations to be more productive (Microsoft's mission is to 'empower every individual and organisation in the world to achieve more'). By working together, there is the potential to create a technology platform that will foster office collaboration, sharing and productivity on a whole new scale.

As a business-to-business (B2B) platform, LinkedIn allows users to create 'connections' with people, who can then build up a professional network of contacts comprising 1$^{st}$, 2$^{nd}$ and 3rd-degree connections.

- 1st-degree - People you're directly connected to because you have accepted their invitation to connect, or they have accepted your invitation.
- 2nd-degree - People who are connected to your 1st-degree connections.
- 3rd-degree - People who are connected to your 2nd-degree connections.

You can find out about LinkedIn news and product updates via their blog: business.linkedin.com/en-uk/marketing-solutions/blog.

# Twitter

Twitter: fast and concise in its messaging, this social media platform can work well for both businesses and individuals. Founded in 2006, Twitter's mission is 'to give everyone the power to create and share ideas and information instantly, without barriers'. The power of Twitter lies in finding prospects based on what they tell the world about themselves – in their Twitter bio or in the Tweets they share. In 2016 Twitter relaxed its 140 characters-per-tweet rule to allow users to add pictures, videos and to mention other users without eating into their limit.

As Twitter is a public network, all Tweets can appear in search engine results: a search engine might not find your website against a set of search terms, but it might find your Tweets on such matters. The public nature of the network also makes it a great platform for being able to listen to, and gain valuable insights into, your audience, your customers and your competitors (see Chapter 5 for more on this).

The hashtag (#) is one of the most powerful social media features. First used in a Tweet in 2007, hashtags help group conversations around keywords, phrases and topics. In 2009 Twitter formally adopted the use of hashtags into code, automatically hyperlinking terms using the # sign. Check out **hashtags.org** and **hashtagify.me** to find which ones are relevant to you, your business and your targeted audiences.

To keep up to date with Twitter news, visit blog.twitter.com.

# Facebook

Founded in 2004, Facebook's stated mission is 'to give people the power to share and make the world more open and connected. People use Facebook to stay connected with friends and family, to discover what's going on in the world, and to share and express what matters to them.'

First launched as a social networking service for Harvard University students, Facebook arrived in the UK in 2005, again targeted at students. The network opened to the public in September 2006. It has provided unprecedented insights into people's lives and psychology.

On the Facebook platform, individuals have 'profiles' and businesses have 'pages'. The visibility of posts to those who follow (or 'like') your Facebook page can depend on popularity and advertising spend.

Facebook tends to be more effective for organisations operating in a business-to-consumer (B2C) market, rather than business-to-business, although peer-to-peer conversation in private groups is increasingly popular.

For Facebook news and product updates, visit newsroom.fb.com/news.

## Instagram

The photo and video sharing app, Instagram, launched in October 2010, and was acquired by Facebook in September 2012. In 2016, Instagram added business accounts that have functionality for targeting, measurement and reporting.

Instagram's goal is to help companies reach their respective audiences through captivating imagery in a rich, visual environment, and is used most effectively by image-friendly businesses. From Instagram, it is easy to share pictures (instantly) across multiple platforms, including Facebook and Twitter.

Instagram news and updates can be found at instagram.com/press.

## Google+

Google+ didn't appear until June 2011, by which time LinkedIn, Facebook and Twitter had established themselves and were generating business results. It had a hesitant start, with many accounts being created 'by default' (when setting up a Google account for other services such as Gmail). However, the SEO and web traffic benefits of Google+ have allowed it to survive, in somewhat different formats. The 'new' Google+ was announced in November 2015 and focuses on interests, communities and collections. It is used primarily by business-to-business and technology-focused businesses.

For all Google updates, see googleblog.blogspot.co.uk.

• • •

## How to choose which social media platform to use

Knowing which social media platform will work best for you and your business is not straightforward. You might be tempted to go for the platform you find easiest to use, but this might not always be the best option. You might also be tempted to try them all, but that's nigh on impossible and will not make the best use of any resources you have available (particularly time). When we read about the size and growth of social media platforms, we might be inspired to get involved. However, size doesn't always matter: the platforms with the most users won't necessarily be best for our business.

When deciding what social media platform(s) to use, there are a number of key questions to ask:

- **What do you want to achieve?**
  Are you looking to create brand awareness, drive traffic to your website to generate leads, or provide customer services? In Chapter 2 we'll look at each of these areas in more detail.
- **Where is your target audience?**
  Demographic information is always available for each platform – there can be some key trends by age and gender. But, more importantly, how many of your prospects and customers use the platform? We will review this question in more detail in Chapter 4.
- **What are your competitors doing?**
  Which platforms are they using, and do you need to be there too? Are there opportunities they are missing that you could take advantage of? We will look at competitor monitoring in Chapter 4.
- **What type of content do you have to share?**
  Some platforms suit all content types, but others are more specific (e.g. video only). If you will be sharing time-sensitive updates frequently, Twitter might be good for you. But if you will be sharing a few updates once or twice every week, LinkedIn might be a better option. We'll talk more about content types in Chapter 6.

There's no precise set of rules to determine which social media platforms will be best for you and your business, so carefully consider the questions, the nature of each platform, and your resources (see Figure 1.2).

- **Should you be on LinkedIn?** Yes, if you are a business professional.
- **Should you be on Twitter?** Yes, if you are sharing 'in the moment' news and want to take part in fast-paced topical discussions.

- **Should you be on Facebook?** Yes, if you are in a business-to-consumer industry such as travel, food, hospitality, leisure or retail, or wish to take part in peer-to-peer conversations in an informal setting.
- **Should you be on Instagram?** Yes, if your business is image-friendly and you can share the human side (or 'behind the scenes' information) of your business.
- **Should you be on Google+?** Yes, if you want to impact your SEO, and if you are serving a business-to-business and/or technology-focused audience.

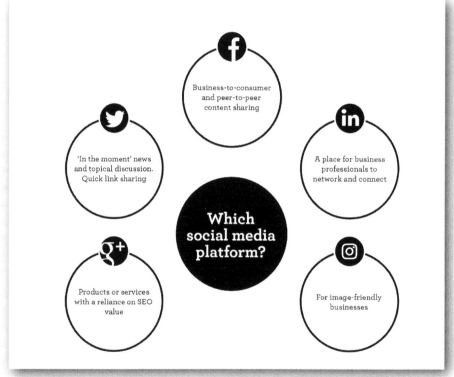

*Figure 1.2. At-a-glance guide to the 'big 5' social networking platforms.*

# Relax!

- Technology, and social media, enable us to do everything we've always done – just faster, and with greater reach. The mobile revolution has given us more power.
- There's really nothing unique about social media for you and your business to fear. It's just another channel. Change is inevitable. People will talk about you. Employees will leave your business. Don't fear social media because of this.
- Just like television and radio, social media is a channel for communication. It is new, but it has not replaced traditional channels. Indeed, social media works best when it is integrated with other channels, and across business functions.
- Thinking about the above questions will help you decide which social media platform(s) are most appropriate for you and your business. Don't try to do it all. Focus on what you want to achieve, and where you can find your target audience.

# CHAPTER 2
## What's the point of social media?

© Clarketoons.com

In this chapter we take the first steps towards understanding how to make social media work for you and your business. We start with *why*. We learn about the different types of social media user, the functional building blocks that help us make sense of social media, and the different platforms available. Most importantly, we identify that social media is *not* a strategy.

> The answers are all out there. We just
> need to ask the right questions.
> OSCAR WILDE

Making social media work for you and your business is not easy. Many businesses, large and small, have taken to using social media without first making a plan. I often hear 'we gave it a try' and 'it doesn't work'. After a little probing, it turns out the trial took place without a plan and with no understanding of what success would look like.

Lewis Carroll put it perfectly when he said: 'If you don't know where you're going, any road will get you there.' The key is to be specific about what you want to achieve. It could be that you want to get more clients for your business, increase traffic to your website, get more enquiries through your website, and so on. As you will read later in this chapter, social media can help do all of those things, but starting with social media as the solution is a big mistake. You need to start with *why*.

## Start with why

Grab a coffee, sit down and find Simon Sinek's 'Start with Why' TED talk on YouTube. Bookmark it, buy the book, and return to it whenever you're faced with a new business challenge.

Sinek says that every organisation functions on three levels:

1. What we do.
2. How we do it.
3. Why we do it.

Sinek argues that every organisation knows what it does – the products it sells or services it offers, and every individual knows what they do – their job title and responsibilities. Some also know how they do what they do and what they think makes them different from everyone else. However, Sinek continues, few people and organisations can clearly articulate *why* they do what they do – and why that should matter to anyone else.

**What**
Every organization on the planet knows WHAT they do. These are products they sell or the services they offer.

**How**
Some organizations know HOW they do it. These are the things that make them special or set them apart from their competition.

**Why**
Very few organizations know WHY they do what they do. WHY is not about winning a Greek Week contest or Buchanan Cup. That's a result. It's a purpose, cause or belief. It's the very reason your organisation exsists.

*Figure 2.1. The 'Golden Circle'. Image reproduced with permission from the author.*

Sinek calls this concept the 'Golden Circle' (see Figure 2.1). Most of the time we communicate from the outside in. We start with what we do, then how we do it.

Compare the following examples provided by Sinek ('The Golden Circle: Presenter Slides & Notes').

|  | Example 1 |
|---|---|
| What | Here is our law firm |
| How | We have the industry's most intelligent lawyers, who graduated from the world's top schools. Have you seen our client list? Only from the Fortune 500! And, check out our offices – they are absolutely pristine. |
| Behaviour | Come do business with our law firm! |

|         | Example 2 |
|---------|-----------|
| Why     | We believe in servicing the needs of others so that they can focus on the difference they need to make. |
| How     | We do so by bringing on some of the most intelligent legal professionals who graduated from the world's top schools. We work with top performing organisations, most of which are on the Fortune 500 list, so that we can help them make a larger difference in the world. And, we like to go above and beyond, so we have built pristine offices. |
| What    | We are a world-class law firm. Come see for yourself. |

If asked why they choose one product or service over the other, the decision-maker often cites the features, benefits, facts or figures, because the neocortex, the thinking part of the brain, is always trying to understand and make sense of the world. This is why we think we are rational beings when we are really not. People understand factual information – but this understanding does not drive behaviour. If it did, we would never buy a product or service simply because of how it makes us feel. We would never be loyal; we would always choose the best deal. We would never care about trust or relationships; we would only evaluate the numbers. We don't do that. We choose a product, service or company over another because of the way it makes us feel. Consider the last big purchase you made: why did you select that company's product or service?

By contrast, when we communicate from the inside out – starting with why – communication starts to drive decision-making and behaviour, attracting people with reciprocal beliefs and who want to be a part of the same cause.

> People don't buy what you do, they buy why you do it.
> SIMON SINEK

So, for the Golden Circle to work properly you must be clear about *why*, be disciplined about *how* and be consistent about *what*. No one section is more important than the other. The most important thing is a balance across all three. When an individual or organisation is clear about its purpose or its 'why', everyone, from employees to customers, can understand it.

If you want help discovering your why, visit Sinek's website, startwithwhy. com.

Now we know our *why*, we can get back to social media …

## The six types of social media user

Before committing to using social media, and any specific platform, we must also consider our audience. In Chapter 4 we will talk in more detail about finding our audience, but for now let's consider some different 'types' of social media users.

At the end of 2011, loyalty management firm Aimia conducted research in the USA ('Staring at the Sun: Identifying, Understanding and Influencing Social Media Users') that identified six social media 'personas':

- **No-shows** – those who have not logged on to a social network in the past 30 days. 'A typical 'no-show' exhibits a low degree of trust, and has no interest in broadcasting his/her activities or interests to anyone.'
- **Newcomers** – 'typically passive users of a single social media network. A passive user may reluctantly join Facebook, for example, in order not to feel "left behind". Newcomers primarily use social media to enhance their offline relationships.'
- **Onlookers** – these users 'may lurk on several social media networks, but post infrequently. They rely on social media primarily to keep up on the online lives of others within their social networks, but are reluctant to share details about themselves.'
- **Cliquers** are 'active, single-network users who congregate primarily on Facebook. Most of their online sharing includes photos, status updates and comments. Within their small network of close friends and family, they're active and influential.'
- **Mix-n-minglers** – the largest group of social media users – participate actively on multiple social networking platforms.

They 'like to follow brands in order to receive offers and keep up with the latest news. Within their network of friends, they're influential – and they meet many of these friends online.'

- **Sparks** 'are the most active and deeply engaged users of social media.' Sparks 'engage with brands frequently, and will serve as enthusiastic ambassadors for their favourites.'

What type of social media user are you? What type of social media user would you like to be? It's OK to be any of these. If it matches your objective to solely use social media for research and intelligence, you can be an onlooker. If you want to actively participate, then mix 'n' mingle!

• • •

Now that you've established why you do what you do, and have considered what sort of social media users your ideal customers are, you can consider the features offered by different social media platforms and decide which will be the best fit for you, your business, your aims, and your customers.

## The honeycomb of social media

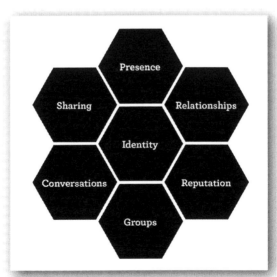

*Figure 2.2. The honeycomb of social media (Kietzmann et al 2011).*
*Image reproduced with permission from the author.*

Jan H. Kietzmann, Kristopher Hermkens, Ian P. McCarthy and Bruno S. Silvestre provide a useful framework (Figure 2.2) that defines social media by using seven functional building blocks: identity, conversations, sharing, presence, relationships, reputation, and groups.

The seven blocks can be used to explain social media by the extent to which the individual platforms focus on some or all of these blocks. Used individually, or together, the blocks can help managers make sense of social media, and understand their audience and their engagement needs. The blocks are not mutually exclusive, and nor do they all have to be present.

- **Identity** – the extent to which users reveal their identities in a social media setting. People often share personal information freely on social media (such as their name, age, gender, profession, location), but also care how other parties use this information. Understanding the data privacy controls for each of the social media platforms is essential in getting the balance right: all users should read the terms and conditions when setting up an account, and should review privacy and settings regularly. As discussed in Chapter 3, the 'identity' building block is core to creating a good first impression and building brand awareness.
- **Conversations** – the extent to which users communicate with each other in a social media setting. While social media networking platforms are built for conversations, their formats can differ. For example, the pace of a conversation on Twitter is very fast, and messages are very short. Organisations need to be aware of when and how they engage in conversations and when a response is expected or appropriate. We discuss this further in Chapter 5.
- **Sharing** – the extent to which users exchange, distribute and receive content. Sharing is a way of interacting, and may or may not lead to a conversation or relationship. For example, Instagram is all about image-sharing; there is little more text than a caption and keywords (hashtags). Organisations should take care to outline what content can/cannot be shared via social media (see the section on managing risk in Chapter 8).
- **Presence** – the extent to which users know if others are available. This can happen through status lines such as

'available' or location 'check-ins'. If users are engaging in real-time conversations (e.g. instant messaging), this can be useful. Presence is closely linked to other building blocks, particularly conversations and relationships. It should be recognised that social media presence is influenced by the intimacy and immediacy of the relationship, and that higher levels of social media presence are likely to make conversations more influential.

- **Relationships** – the extent to which users relate to each other (that is, where two or more users have some form of association that leads them to converse, share content or simply list each other as a friend). In some cases these relationships are formal and structured – for example, the 1st, 2nd and 3rd degrees of connections on LinkedIn. On other platforms, such as Twitter, the relationship does not need to be reciprocated. Along with presence, the strength of a user's relationship can indicate the likelihood of that user being an influencer in their network. We discuss influencers in Chapter 5.

- **Reputation** – the extent to which users know the social standing of others, including themselves, in a social media setting. In most cases reputation is a matter of trust. It can refer not only to people and their audiences, but also to their content, and how often it is 'liked' or shared. We will discuss reputation management in Chapter 5 and audience and engagement metrics in Chapter 7.

- **Groups** – the extent to which users can form communities or sub-communities. The more 'social' a network becomes, the bigger the group of friends, followers and connections it can involve. Kietzmann et al. (2011) cite a popular relationship-group metric known as Dunbar's Number. Dunbar (2010) theorised that people have a cognitive limit which restricts the number of social relationships they can have with people to around 150. Social media platforms have communities that extend well beyond this limit, and offer tools that allow users to order their connections into groups – for example Google+ circles; they also provide ways to create groups, such as on Facebook and LinkedIn. Groups on social media platforms are more than just lists of users; they are often very active communities that hold conversations on specific topics. Groups can be open to all, or restricted (invitation only or subject to approval).

As you might expect of the 'big 5' social networking platforms, all are strong on identity, reputation and sharing. Facebook and Google+ have a strong 'presence' block, with a feature of knowing who is online and active. Relationships, conversation and groups are strong for Facebook, LinkedIn and Google+. Figure 2.3 shows the focus of the 'big 5' social networking platforms on each of the building blocks.

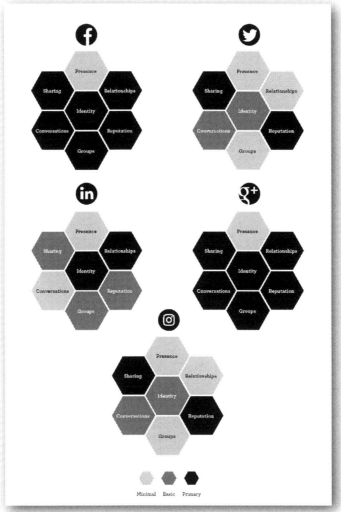

Figure 2.3. How the honeycomb social media model can be applied to the 'big 5' platforms. Images reproduced with permission from the author (Kietzmann et al, 2011).

## What's the big idea?

*Image used with permission of the artist.*

I love this cartoon. I'm a big fan of Tom Fishburne, the Marketoonist, because his observations are realistic and relevant.

Anyone starting an enquiry with 'Let's use Twitter', 'We need to have a Facebook page' or 'Can you show me how to …' is in the wrong place. You've got to start with why you want to use social media, and understand different types of social media user, and the nature and strengths of different social media platforms. Social media might be the best way to enable an organisation to achieve its goals/objectives, but 'We're going digital' is not the place to start. It's not the big idea. Digital is not a strategy; it's a channel.

Let me explain.

The word 'strategy' is so often misused. Just because something's important (or new and shiny) doesn't automatically mean that it is a strategy. The origins of strategy and tactics lie in military definitions: strategy represents the overall approach, the direction that should be taken, and/or the results that should be achieved. Tactics are the manoeuvres used to achieve the strategic objectives, such as a surprise attack or surrounding the enemy.

When applied to business, strategy is the approach you take to achieve your long-term objectives, based on an understanding of your organisation and its operating environment (internal and external). Strategy defines what the business aims to achieve.

And now, let's go back to the Lewis Carroll quote I mentioned at the beginning of the chapter: how do you get 'there', if you don't know where 'there' is?

A *strategy* begins with understanding where you are now and where you want to be. Only once you know where 'there' is can you work out the best route to success. It's clear, therefore, that strategy must precede planning.

A *plan* is the detailed set of short-term activities that includes specific objectives and tactics that support the strategy. A plan is about output. A plan is about *how* you're going to achieve the strategy.

**Social media is *not* a strategy.**

According to Jack Welch, former CEO, General Electric, 'A strategy is something like, an innovative new product; globalisation, taking your product around the world; be the low-cost producer. A strategy is something you can touch; you can motivate people with; be number one and number two in every business. You can energise people around the message.'

A business may have a plan for how to use social media, but it does not have a 'social media strategy'. I'm certain no business ever had a 'fax strategy' or 'leaflet drop strategy'. An approach, an action or a goal can, however, be described as strategic, as they relate back to a business strategy, but they are not *the* strategy. They are the detail of the plan.

Here are two examples to illustrate this point.

Strategy:    To acquire new customers, and to ensure repeat purchases by
             existing customers
Objective:   To increase sales of a certain product by x% by a certain
             date
Tactic:      To publish special offers on Twitter

Strategy:    To identify, develop and recruit new donors, in the age group
             18–25
Objective:   To raise £x for a certain cause by a certain date
Tactic:      To run a targeted advertising campaign on Facebook

In order to find out whether or not you have achieved your strategy, you must ensure your objectives meet SMART criteria. That is, they should be **S**pecific, **M**easurable, **A**chievable, **R**elevant and **T**ime-related. We will look at ways to measure success in greater detail in Chapter 7.

> The essence of strategy is choosing what not to do.
> MICHAEL PORTER

It is important to note that strategy is all about making a choice. There is no 'one size fits all' solution, and a variety of routes can be taken to reach your destination. As we will discuss in Chapter 4, you need to focus on your defined target audience and you also need to tailor your activities according to circumstances and resources. You need to find the best strategic fit. That's when social media works.

Now, let's see how social media might help you realise those goals.

## So, what's the point of social media?

Social media can provide a number of benefits for both you and your business, from brand awareness to lead generation and direct sales. Let's take a look at some of these core objectives.

## Brand awareness

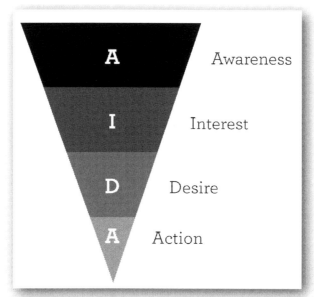

*Figure 2.4. The AIDA model.*

The 'father of advertising', David Ogilvy, defined a brand as 'the intangible sum of a product's attributes: its name, packaging, and price, its history, its reputation, and the way it is advertised'.

The AIDA model (Figure 2.4) can be applied to communications activities, and awareness is the first step. *Awareness* must generate sufficient *interest* in the benefits of a product or service to encourage a prospective customer to research it further. As the customer learns more, s/he builds an emotional connection with the product and moves from 'liking it' to 'wanting' it (*desire*). They then move a step closer towards purchase (*action*).

• • •

Personal branding is now as important as company branding. Whatever field your business operates in, people prefer to connect with a person, not a logo. Think of Richard Branson and Virgin. Think of Mark Zuckerberg and Facebook. With effort and focus, any individual can build a valuable online social presence.

Being present in the right place, at the right time, is important. Presenting yourself, and your business, professionally is paramount. Online content is king, and engaging in conversation is a vital exercise. More on this in Chapter 3.

## Customer service

Social media has changed the way customers and companies interact. Online conversations take place in real time, 24 hours a day. As a channel of communication, social media is excellent for enriching customer experiences, and enabling customer service. It can be used to answer questions, respond to feedback, and to build loyalty. Social media customer service is discussed further in Chapter 5.

## Customer insight and market intelligence

In Chapter 5 you will see that another benefit to social media listening is insight and market intelligence. Social media provides real-time insights into what your ideal customers are thinking and saying. Social media is an easy way to learn about your audience, and it's also less expensive than traditional market research methods such as surveys and focus groups. Listening does not need to be confined to audiences; you can also use it to gain key information on competitors – who they are, what content they are sharing, what their customers are saying about them, and so on.

## Lead generation and direct sales

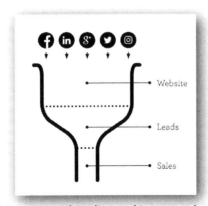

*Figure 2.5. How social media can drive your sales process.*

Lead generation is about bringing people into your sales process (Figure 2.5). This often starts with a visit to your website. Social media can make this easy – if you understand your audience and know what platforms they use, you can listen in to conversations and find business leads. If you make connections and stay at the front of their minds you will be recalled when the time is right for them to purchase. If you share content that your audience finds interesting and relevant to their needs, they will engage with you. Every post on a social media platform can provide an opportunity to demonstrate your expertise and add value, moving prospective customers one step along the path to purchase (*action*). We'll discuss social selling in Chapter 5.

## Recruitment

Social media humanises a brand like never before. Some organisations use social media, particularly the more visual platforms (such as Instagram), to highlight what goes on 'behind the scenes' or other relevant elements of an organisation's culture; employer branding factors are particularly important to supporting the recruitment process.

In *Social Media Recruitment: How to Successfully Integrate Social Media into Recruitment Strategy* (p. 23) Andy Headworth explains: 'Due to the proliferation of different social media networks and the associated tools and platforms using the social data, social media can be used across the whole recruitment lifecycle … sourcing, attraction, application, selection, on-boarding, during employment and when an employee leaves the company.' Headworth believes that social media is a vital part of any recruitment strategy.

## Relax!

- Watch Simon Sinek's famous TED talk and determine your *why*. Write it down.
- Consider what type of social media user you are right now, and what you would like to be. Throughout this book, consider what

type of social media user your target audience might be, and how you might best find, and build relationships with, them.

- When we talk about social media, we are really talking about what we *do* on social media (not the platforms themselves). There are a number of business benefits to using social media, including building brand awareness, improving customer service, lead generation, recruitment, and gaining insights into your marketplace.
- Know your business strategy and objectives. Decide which objectives social media can help deliver.
- Remember, social media does not operate in a vacuum – it supports, enhances or amplifies several business functions, including marketing, customer service and human resources.

# CHAPTER 3
## Making a good first impression

© Clarketoons.com

The web is your Hollywood agent, speaking for you whenever you are not around. It's so important to make a good first impression, but all too often profiles are set up quickly and never revisited. This chapter contains advice on how to get it right, so you're ready to do business.

> You never get a second chance to make a first impression.
> WILL ROGERS

In the real world, we spend time preparing to make a good first impression: for example, in the way we dress for a job interview or a first date. However, online we're often a little, well, lazier. We create an account, fill in a few boxes with our details, and walk away until we need something, such as a new job!

Not spending time completing and updating your social media profiles is a huge mistake, but it's made by so many people. Would you leave the house half-dressed if you were attending a business meeting? It's just the same with online profiles.

Checking out someone's social media profiles before I meet them is one of my favourite parts of training and presenting. I love being able to recognise someone from their profile picture so I can greet them by name. It's interesting when I hold up LinkedIn profile printouts and see people recoil into their seat, impressed that I have done my homework, but also embarrassed at what I've seen. I put the first reaction – recoiling – down to being terribly British, but we should be proud, not ashamed, of our achievements. The second reaction – embarrassment – is because people suddenly realise that we should take more control of the information we share about ourselves online, because it's globally visible and because it really matters if we want to make a good first impression and start to build relationships.

Once a first impression has been made, it is extremely hard to change. On social media you have even less time to make an impact than if you were meeting face-to-face. A social media profile is like a job interview that takes place in under ten seconds. Amazon CEO Jeff Bezos says: 'Your brand is what people say about you when you're not in the room.' Your online profile is your brand representative, so it's vital to get it right, and to keep it up-to-date.

Social media profiles are your shop window, so you need to make sure they are dressed to create trust, demonstrate professionalism, and show your readiness to do business.

Because the first impression you make is the main way for someone to find out if you are able to give them what they want or need (i.e., can you solve their problem?), you also need to focus on content. No matter how great you are, if you cannot show how you can be helpful, add value, or that you are credible and trustworthy, the relationship will be a non-starter. Also, if people search and find you, take a look at you and think, 'You look OK, let's go further', do they see that you are active, do you share content that is inspiring or useful, or do they find endless cat pictures and negative comments? Content matters, and we'll discuss this in more detail in Chapter 6.

## Ten steps to success

To help put this chapter into context, here are my ten steps to social networking success:

1. Your target audience is searching for someone like you.
2. Your profile matches their search criteria, and appears high in the search results.
3. Your picture and headline stand out (as professional) in the search results.
4. They click through to your profile.
5. They get a good sense of who you are, what you do, and how you can help them.
6. They read your testimonials and see how you might already be connected (friends, colleagues etc.).
7. They start to trust you.
8. They send you a LinkedIn connection request, add you to their Google+ network, like your Facebook page, or follow you on Twitter or Instagram.
9. You reciprocate the connection/like/follow.
10. You stay in front of them regularly, engage in conversation – and do business together when the time is right.

## The power of Google

If first impressions count, then you are who Google says you are.

Open up a new browser window and search for your own name. See what information appears, and in what order (people will usually only look at the first results). Are you happy with the information you see? If not, make an immediate list of actions you could take to rectify the situation, starting with removing inappropriate pictures and checking your privacy settings.

Keywords have been an important factor in online marketing for a number of years. Anyone with a website will be familiar with search engine optimisation (SEO), in which keywords play a large part. But keywords – the words and phrases people are using to search for something – are also an important part of social media activity. They are essential to getting our profiles found. For guidance on how to carry out keyword research, visit my website luanwise.co.uk/how-i-help.

Search for your keywords on Google and other search engines. Do your social media profiles appear in the first page of search results? Next, search for those keywords on each of the social media platforms you intend to use – where do you appear? Who else appears? Make a list of where you are now, and other profiles that appear high on search results, as it's useful information to use when optimising your own profile.

## Keeping it real (usernames)

Social media is social. It's about people (remember, technology is just the facilitator), and people want to do business with people, not faceless businesses. So, on your social media profiles, be yourself and keep it real with sensible usernames and claim your own URL.

- As a default, most social media platforms attach a random string of numbers or letters to your URL when you first set up a profile: for example, uk.linkedin.com/luan-wise-3a4943121. I have personalised my URL to be uk.linkedin.com/in/luanwise.

A personalised, or vanity, URL is not only easy to remember, and neater when sharing on email signatures, business cards and other literature, but it also helps with that all-important search results position because, after all, you're using social media to get you and your business found, right? (If for some reason you do not wish your profiles to appear in search engine results, go to the privacy settings on the individual platforms where you can switch them off).

When setting up profiles, consider setting up a separate profile for yourself (professionally), and your business. Some social media platforms have different options for business profiles. For example:

- Facebook profiles are for individuals
- Facebook pages are for businesses (and are set up from an individual's profile; there can be a number of administrators)
- LinkedIn profiles are for individuals
- LinkedIn company pages are for businesses (and are administered by nominated employees)
- Instagram introduced business accounts in 2016. These have added reported functionality, but are currently no different in set-up or appearance
- Google+ profiles are for individuals
- Google+ business accounts are for businesses (and are set up from an individual's profile; there can be a number of administrators). There are different options depending on whether your business has a physical presence, or not.

Personal and corporate accounts should interact sensibly. My recommendation is that, as part of an agreed social media policy (see Chapter 8), corporate content should be driven from the core (company) accounts, and then shared by individuals on their personal profiles. This allows company pages to act as a single content hub, and individuals can leverage their own, often larger, personal networks to achieve maximum reach.

## Multiple accounts

In training sessions or presentations, people often ask me whether it's acceptable to have multiple accounts on a single social media platform. The answer is that it depends on the platform. Individuals should only have one Facebook profile and one LinkedIn profile (as per their terms and conditions). A business can have a LinkedIn company page, and use showcase pages for specific products, brands or business units. Over time, changes made to Google products has meant some existing users inadvertently created multiple Google+ accounts; my advice is to try and keep your interaction with Google+ as simple as possible, with just one profile and one business account.

Many organisations opt for multiple Twitter and Instagram accounts or Facebook pages. People like to follow accounts that post topics that interest them, so if you have disparate messages to send, creating separate accounts can be a great way to show a human side to a business and be more relevant to the various needs of your audiences.

On these social media platforms you could consider having:

- **a corporate account** – specifically dedicated to providing updates on your company as a whole
- **a customer service account** – a profile to answer questions and comments
- **a product-led account** – to provide product news and information: for example, retailers could have separate accounts for menswear and womenswear
- **audience-led accounts** – focused on the needs of a target audience: for example, this could be location-specific if your business is international, or subject-specific for higher education establishments.

For Twitter, consider asking key individuals within your business to Tweet. For example, messages straight from the CEO can work well.

It's great for thought leadership positioning and for raising your brand's profile. Richard Branson is excellent at this. If you have a number of customer-facing staff members, consider a unified approach to usernames, such as @CompanynameJohn, @CompanynameSarah, etc. I believe that people-led accounts are important in building trust and relationships, but should not replace a corporate Twitter account. As with LinkedIn company pages and personal profiles, the corporate Twitter account should be the 'content hub', with further sharing taking place across personal accounts.

As well as needing to have the time and resource to manage multiple accounts, it is important to establish whether you have an audience and a need for multiple accounts before setting them up. If you're not sure how to progress, take a look at what your competitors are doing. Do they have multiple accounts? Also, review the type of responses and messages you are receiving from your audiences – what do they need from you? If you think it might be too complex to manage multiple accounts, consider how you might unify your content (we'll discuss content planning in Chapter 6).

CASE STUDY

For example, I once facilitated a workshop at an event venue to discuss its social media presence. The venue hosted a variety of events from weddings to corporate conferences. To create multiple Twitter accounts for each type of event would be too time-consuming to manage, but to share wedding information alongside information on corporate events could alienate an audience. The workshop concluded by deciding to focus content-sharing on the venue, to emphasise its versatility. It's a well-known venue in the local area, so to highlight 'what's on' and key features such as food, staff and service, which make the venue the right choice for any occasion, the Twitter account could stay manageable and meet the interests of a wider audience.

• • •

Smaller businesses, however, sometime integrate the business brand with the personal brand of the owner. Remember, all decisions should be co-ordinated with the business's strategy and objectives when planning the use of social media (as discussed in Chapter 2). Do what works for you, your business and your audience.

## Smile for the camera (profile pictures)

I could fill a whole book with awful social media profile pictures! It's amazing that an element so under the control of the user can be so bad. The visuals on your profile really do matter. We may not like the idea of being judged by our appearance, but it's how people work. Visuals stand out from text, and have a major impact on the first impression of you and your business. There should be no family, friends, colleagues, pets, wedding or party outfits in professional social media profile pictures. Even on profiles used personally (e.g. Facebook), take the time to consider your profile picture, as it can often be discovered via Google image search. Keep your shop window professional at all times, please!

Not having a photo can also hamper your interactions on social media – according to LinkedIn, a profile with a photo receives 14 times more views than a profile without a photo. People do business with people, so they want to see a professional picture before they follow/make a connection. Don't let a potential business opportunity disappear in a few seconds because your profile picture doesn't look professional or ready for business.

What makes a good photo? A good, clear, up-to-date head and shoulders shot looking at the camera: this helps with connection, as we like to see the eyes of people we see on screen. A smile is nice, as it makes you seem more approachable and trustworthy. Wear business attire that complements your line of business, and use a neutral backdrop that does not distract from the main image. Think about how you might dress if you were being interviewed for your job, or if you were going to meet a potential client for the first time.

Using the same good social media photograph across all social media platforms is recommended for consistency and recognition. Remember, profile pictures can appear at quite a small size, which is why a head and shoulders shot is best, rather than full length. You should use a personal picture on personal profiles and a company logo as your profile picture only where the content is corporately driven.

Don't forget that cover/background images on social media profiles are also important, since they're the largest visual a visitor will see. Make sure the images you use are relevant, professional and at a good-quality resolution.

© Clarketoons.com

## Introducing yourself

If you want people to read or hear your story, you'll need to hook them in with a strong introduction. Your LinkedIn profile headline, your Twitter, Instagram or Google+ bio, your Facebook page 'about' description – they all set expectations, and initiate readers' decisions to make a connection, like or follow a page.

Your headline/bio appears in search results, and is the most visible description of you on the internet. As we saw in the 'ten steps to success', after you have been found, it's the second most important factor. It's the difference between someone clicking through to see the rest of your profile, or scrolling down to the next result.

These short 'elevator pitches' need to clarify what you and your account are all about. They need to answer the 'who', 'what', 'where', 'why' and 'when' for your presence on that specific social media platform. For example, on social media, just like at face-to-face networking events, many people answer the question 'What do you do?' with their job title. Networking expert Will Kintish explains that this is not the most effective way to tell someone what you do. People answering with their job title, such as 'accountant' or 'lawyer' are sharing what they *are*, not what they *do*. The answer to the question should be more people-focused and benefit-led, such as: 'I help people with corporate tax planning' or 'I specialise in advising on R&D tax credits; in fact, I have already saved my clients £1m this year!' Your 'why' is a far better way to approach an introduction, both in real life and online.

You could also consider including a short explanation about what your business does. For example, people may not have heard of 'XYZ Software Ltd', but if you tell them 'XYZ Software Ltd is a world leader in CAD/CAM software development' early on, they can quickly decide if you are the person they are looking to do business with.

Experiment with different headlines/bio descriptions and see what works for you. By 'works', I mean starting with the vanity metrics of number of connections, follows and likes … but in Chapter 8 we will look at how this converts to more meaningful metrics. You can also change your headline/bio descriptions regularly to fit with your business activity. It's OK to do this! Your existing connections are unlikely to pay too much attention, because they already know you – your purpose behind doing this is to make a good first impression on new contacts. For example, if you are pitching for business in a certain industry sector, add 'specialist in the pharmaceutical sector' to your descriptor text for a while. If you're looking for a new job, fill your headline with keywords relating to your areas of specialism. Just make sure your privacy settings are tight, so you don't alert your whole network to your experiments.

You can add links and other usernames in a bio, but I don't recommend it. Before including them, you should consider if they serve a purpose – such as driving traffic to your own website – or whether they could form a distraction and will lead people to click-through to somewhere else, and forget about you! Keep focused on your objectives.

Note: before writing headlines or bios, please check out your social media policy and the guidance that an employer might provide regarding links to corporate accounts and disclosure of your employment status on personal profiles. Take a look at 'managing risk' in Chapter 8.

## Sharing your professional story

LinkedIn reports that only 51% of profiles are filled out. An incomplete profile cuts down your chances of being found. Getting found is the first step to success, a strong introduction is second, then it's down to how you present yourself with information that is credible, authentic, professional and indicates trustworthiness.

Once you have nailed the first impression, you want to make sure the rest of your profile is filled in. Now is your chance to 'show and tell' the detail of your professional business story. You have stepped out of the elevator, and have a bit more time to explain. If you have told someone that you can advise on R&D tax credits, and if that's of some interest to them, they will ask another question and you can begin to elaborate.

Keep your most valuable information at the top of your profile. Your aim is to get people interested and onto your own platform (website) or other form of communication (email, telephone, face-to-face) as soon as possible.

On all of the social media platforms you need to fill in all the information boxes, using your keywords, in as much detail as the character count allows. Be consistent with your story across profiles, but also adapt the information you provide to the nuances of each platform and your objectives for using each of them. For example, I consider LinkedIn to be the social media platform where I'm wearing a business suit (for men, a tie), so my text is more formal. Twitter can be a little more relaxed (ties and jackets off), and with character restrictions it's got to be straight to the point. I use pinned Tweets to support my current work, and use the background visual to add detail to my bio. Facebook pages are akin to an after-work meeting in a bar or coffee shop, so it's more conversational in style. Use the short and long 'about' descriptions in a more relaxed tone than your LinkedIn company page description. At all times, however, you should be professional, authentic, positive and show confidence. Offline and online, you need to have a strong handshake and warm smile whenever you meet someone.

Finally, you can further optimise your profiles by checking out what your competitors are up to. Earlier, you noted down competitors who appeared in search results for your keywords. Examine their profiles – see what you can learn from them and what you can include within your own profile. LinkedIn's 'How you rank for profile views' is great for this. Use the best information, but also make sure you stand out from the crowd.

## Keep it personal, but professional

Personal profiles used for business should stay personal (but be professional). They should focus on you, your achievements, and how you add value to a business relationship (employer, client or supplier). Social media profiles are not the place for a sales pitch. Company pages are where you should showcase product/service information, as well as supporting the human faces of an organisation.

Remember, you cannot be all things to all people, so your profile descriptions should focus on your target audience, by answering their needs/wants. Profiles should be set up to achieve your business strategy and objectives. Just like your username, keep your descriptions real and avoid corporate buzzwords. Be positive – and be honest. You have only one chance at making a first impression, so plan carefully and present yourself and your business in the best way possible.

It's OK to show personality on social media profiles, even when they're used for business. We'll talk later about a 'rule of thirds' for your content (see Chapter 6). In face-to-face meetings where you enter an office, you might look round for family photos, memorabilia, etc. to use to start a conversation. It's OK to do that on social media too – even at work, we're still people with other interests. You need to look for a conversation hook, and provide some information about yourself for others to do the same. For a long time I've used 'shoe lover' and 'caffeine addict' in my social media profiles, and this has sparked conversation, generated meetings and helped convert interest to a sale. I also know that each year I'll catch up with my 'Eurovision buddy', a business editor, on Twitter as we check we've downloaded our scorecards ready for the live show.

## Privacy and settings

When you opened that new browser window to Google yourself, is the information you thought was private actually private? Or did you have a shock when you realised the whole world, including potential clients, colleagues and associates, could see your holiday photos?

On each of the social media platforms, check out what other people can see (there is usually a 'view as' dropdown option on your profile's home page). Use the privacy settings to determine what information you wish to display publicly.

Many of us use social media for personal relationships as well as business purposes. As outlined in Chapter 8, a social media policy can be used to define the line for employees between professional and personal use of social media. To keep worlds apart and information secure, do check your privacy settings. Don't include any personal information you want to stay hidden. For example, can your friends tag you in Facebook photos; can your LinkedIn network see all your business connections?

It's also important to note that, to protect your intellectual property rights, you should register any usernames related to your business name and other trademarks so others cannot use them and, at the same time, make sure your business's social media usernames don't infringe any other businesses' IP rights.

## Relax!

If your ideal client were looking for your product/service, would your profiles encourage them to approach you?

- Go incognito and search for yourself and your business online. Your goal is to have your profile appear at the top of the search engine results page. If you are not happy with the results you see (or don't see), take action to resolve them.
- Carefully consider your introduction. The 120 characters on your LinkedIn personal profile headline, 160 characters on your Twitter bio, 155 characters in your Facebook page short description, 150 characters of your Instagram bio and 77 visible characters on Google+ need to work as hard as possible to give people a snapshot of who you are and what you are about, and show potential contacts that you're credible, trustworthy and able to help them.
- Ensure that you share only the information you want to share by checking your privacy settings for each social media platform you use.
- Stay in control of your online presence and make sure it's always telling the professional story you want it to. Diarise time to review your profiles, at least on a quarterly basis.

# CHAPTER 4
## Finding your audience on social media

© Clarketoons.com

Having a profile and posting some content on social media will not naturally create an audience; you've got to go out and find your audience. You also need to know who you want to be in that audience. You've got to make connections and become known.

Without clear objectives and a thorough understanding of your audience(s) and knowledge about how to influence their behaviour, social media cannot help your business move forward. Simply having a profile will not deliver results.

In Chapter 1 we discussed how to choose which social media platform to use. At the time we considered briefly the nature of each platform, and what type of business purpose it could help achieve. It's now time to add more detail, and ask: Which social media platform/s are going to work best for your audience? This is the most important consideration. After all, we want to be in the place where our audience is most likely to be, and where we're most likely to find people with similar profiles.

In Chapter 3, we looked at making a good first impression. What we didn't cover was: To whom do we wish to make that good first impression? We talked about keywords to help our profile get found, but *who* do we want to find us? Businesses need to know who their customers are in order to find them, reach them and communicate with them effectively.

In Chapter 6 we will talk about content marketing and storytelling. Social media becomes the bridge between content and an audience – without the right audience your content will have no impact; without good, relevant content you will not be able to engage your audience. At the beginning of this book we talked about social media being about technology – as the enabler and the distribution channel – so let's define our audiences, see where we can find them, and later on in the book we will determine what stories to tell them.

## Defining your target audience

Many businesses try to be all things to all people. It can be difficult to understand that not everyone will want to buy your product or service – but could you fulfil the demand for orders if they did?!

*Image used with permission of the artist.*

It's important to have a clear focus on the people we want to target with our product or service; this doesn't stop people from outside that group purchasing from you, but it allows you to target your communications in a way that will resonate more strongly with those who matter most.

Published data can be a useful starting point. Figure 4.1 shows demographic data for Facebook and Twitter users in the UK. Can you match your target audience and the social media platforms you are using with the trends in this data?

Whether your product or service is aimed at a business-to-consumer (B2C) or business-to-business (B2B) audience, it's essential to understand who you are

## UK Facebook User Penetration, by Age, 2014-2020
### % of internet users in each group

|        | 2014  | 2015  | 2016  | 2017  | 2018  | 2019  | 2020  |
|--------|-------|-------|-------|-------|-------|-------|-------|
| 0-11   | 20.6% | 20.9% | 20.7% | 20.6% | 20.4% | 20.4% | 20.4% |
| 12-17  | 79.5% | 79.6% | 79.0% | 78.3% | 76.6% | 74.9% | 72.7% |
| 18-24  | 87.4% | 87.2% | 86.4% | 85.6% | 84.9% | 84.3% | 83.5% |
| 25-34  | 81.1% | 80.1% | 79.2% | 78.3% | 77.4% | 76.5% | 76.1% |
| 35-44  | 69.4% | 70.1% | 70.9% | 71.6% | 71.6% | 71.5% | 71.0% |
| 45-54  | 58.4% | 60.6% | 62.7% | 63.9% | 65.3% | 66.7% | 68.1% |
| 55-64  | 48.8% | 52.4% | 53.5% | 54.2% | 54.9% | 55.5% | 55.9% |
| 65+    | 33.8% | 38.8% | 41.5% | 43.2% | 45.1% | 47.3% | 49.4% |
| **Total** | **61.3%** | **62.2%** | **62.5%** | **62.5%** | **62.4%** | **62.5%** | **62.6%** |

Note: internet users who access their Facebook account via any device at least once per month
Source: eMarketer, Feb 2016

204915                                                    www.**eMarketer**.com

## UK Twitter User Penetration, by Age, 2014-2020
### % of internet users in each group

|        | 2014  | 2015  | 2016  | 2017  | 2018  | 2019  | 2020  |
|--------|-------|-------|-------|-------|-------|-------|-------|
| 0-11   | 3.7%  | 4.3%  | 4.6%  | 4.7%  | 4.9%  | 5.1%  | 5.2%  |
| 12-17  | 34.2% | 37.0% | 39.1% | 40.5% | 41.4% | 41.9% | 42.0% |
| 18-24  | 48.9% | 51.6% | 53.8% | 55.8% | 58.2% | 59.9% | 60.8% |
| 25-34  | 36.3% | 38.1% | 40.1% | 40.9% | 42.7% | 43.6% | 44.5% |
| 35-44  | 29.3% | 31.3% | 33.3% | 35.4% | 36.7% | 38.0% | 38.8% |
| 45-54  | 18.4% | 20.4% | 22.5% | 24.4% | 25.7% | 27.0% | 28.3% |
| 55-64  | 10.8% | 12.2% | 13.0% | 13.5% | 14.0% | 14.5% | 14.9% |
| 65+    | 5.6%  | 7.3%  | 8.7%  | 9.8%  | 11.0% | 12.1% | 13.2% |
| **Total** | **23.9%** | **25.5%** | **26.9%** | **27.9%** | **28.9%** | **29.7%** | **30.4%** |

Note: internet users who access their Twitter account via any device at least once per month
Source: eMarketer, Feb 2016

204921                                                    www.**eMarketer**.com

Figure 4.1. Facebook and Twitter user penetration in the UK.
Images used with permission from eMarketer.

talking to, and what makes them tick. Remember you are targeting *people* (some of whom might just happen to be at work). While demographics such as age and gender are important, there are a few other key areas to review:

- **What do they do?** Occupation, level of seniority, responsibilities.
- **Where do they do it?** Geographical location.
- **What they do offline** – lifestyle signals such as where they like to shop, where they prefer to eat, what media they consume (TV channels, radio stations, newspapers, etc.), and which hobbies they participate in.
- **What they do online** – which websites do they visit, which email newsletters do they receive, which social media platforms do they use, etc.

There are many sources for this type of insight, including Mintel, Nielson and YouGov, to name but a few. Links are included in the resource section at the end of the book.

For B2B target audiences, there are some additional criteria to consider. They include:

- business activity (i.e. industry type)
- business size (by turnover, number of employees)
- business type (legal status)
- year of incorporation (i.e. how long they have been trading).

This information can usually be obtained from Companies House.

It is also likely that your business will have more than one target audience to reach out to, each with its own characteristics and communications plan. By no means are all audience groups equal; they need to be considered separately, matched to the business strategy, and prioritised accordingly. Take, for example, the various audiences a university needs to consider (see Figure 4.2) – and this doesn't even include all the different subjects on offer! Take some time now to list your business's different target audiences. Think about current customers, potential customers, media, suppliers and influencers.

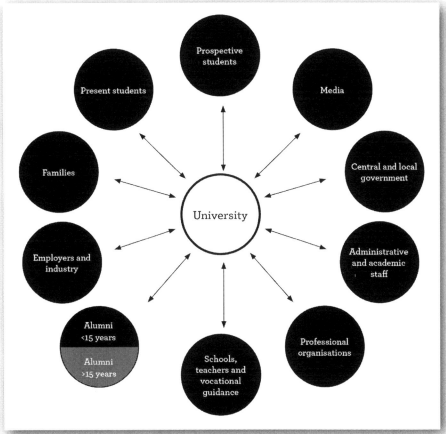

*Figure 4.2. The multiple target audiences of a university.*

## Personas

Any activity that needs to appeal to a target audience, with the aim of persuading them to take action, should involve the creation and use of a *persona*. A persona is a representation of a particular audience segment and are used to help you to understand your audience, specifically:

- their needs (what goals they are trying to achieve) and pain points (their challenges)
- what is important to them
- how best we can communicate with them
- what or who might influence their decision-making.

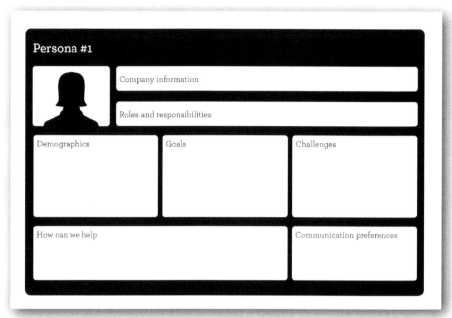

*Figure 4.3. Persona template.*

There are a number of approaches to preparing personas; one-to-one or group interviews are usually most effective. Create a standard list of questions and explore them during the discussion. Do your own research in advance (see below) and use other data to support the interviews, including your website analytics – where people have visited from, what keywords they used to find you, what they did once they were on your website, etc. Social media listening (Chapter 5) can also provide valuable insights. The more research you can apply to the creation of a persona, the more accurate they become.

Once you have created a persona for each of your target audiences, it will be much easier to focus your marketing activity towards them, and to remember your audience are real people, not statistics. Communicate these throughout your business, or even pin them up on your wall as you get to know your customers better and focus your efforts on communicating with them. Writing a piece of content for a marketing director in a 500-person, £10 million turnover B2B software company is much easier when you can visualise them as individuals. Read more on this in Chapter 6.

## Target audience research

Creating personas often relies on using data for existing customers, working on this logic to find 'more of the same'. This is a typical media selection criterion, and has been used for many years in traditional broadcast and printed media. But how can *you* find 'more of the same'?

While published data is useful, to make the most accurate recommendations for any business I'm working with, I find it best to carry out my own research to confirm which social media platforms are most relevant for an audience.

I find it useful to take internal data – whether that's a 'top customer' list or a list of leads generated at a recent trade show, and manually search for those individuals on each of the social media platforms. After confirming whether they are using the platform, it's possible to delve deeper and look at *how* they are using it – for example, what LinkedIn groups are they members of? What content do they 'like' on Twitter? This takes some time, but it's time well spent, and reliable (and rather fascinating, too!) It's helped me to advise clients which social media platforms will most effectively achieve their objectives.

*Figure 4.4. Screenshot from Facebook Ads Manager.*

Facebook, Twitter, LinkedIn and Instagram have their own advertising options. While I'm not suggesting you have to pay for social media advertising to build your audience (but you can if you have the budget available), simply going through the process of looking at these provides a good guide to the size of your potential target audience on each platform.

Log in and go through the set-up process of creating an ad with specific drill-down options to help you focus on your intended audience. For example, the Facebook Ads Manager (see Figure 4.4) allows you to select an audience using location, age, gender, language, interests and behaviour. To give you an idea of potential reach, each platform will then provide a potential audience size, based on whichever targeting options you add in. Give it a try; it's another way to help determine which social media platform is best for your business.

## Finding accounts to follow

There is an important balance to maintain in building an online audience – quality vs quantity. The more followers, connections and page likes you have, the further your messages will reach. However, if you have followers who do not care about you or your business, they hold no value. Remember, the power of social media lies in the network you create and the relationships you build.

Some platforms rely upon reciprocal relationships to form a connection (e.g. LinkedIn and Facebook profiles), while others can be one-way, such as LinkedIn company pages, Facebook pages, Twitter, Instagram and Google+. It's nice to reciprocate the 'follow', but is not necessary if they do not match your target audience persona. Following to get a follow back is a strong approach to building your audience – when you follow or like someone's profile, they will receive a notification. If your profile is ready to make a good first impression (check this by reading Chapter 3), you should get a follow back.

## Hashtags

As a reminder, a hashtag is the # symbol, used to mark keywords or topics. Hashtags are regularly used on Twitter (two or three per Tweet, on average), Google+ and prolifically on Instagram (Instagram allows for up to 30 hashtags per post). They are rarely used on Facebook, and are being re-introduced to LinkedIn.

Use hashtags to search for people talking about the subjects relevant to you and your business, and then follow those that match your target audience criteria.

# Advanced Search

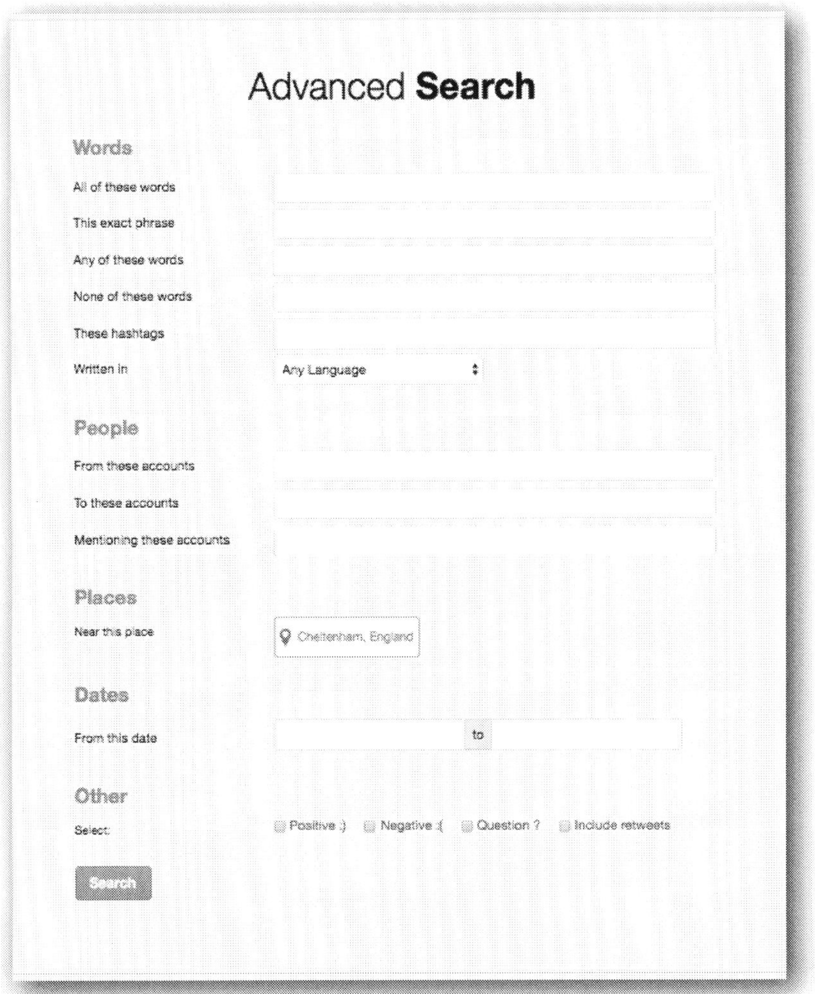

## Advanced **Search**

### Words

All of these words

This exact phrase

Any of these words

None of these words

These hashtags

Written in — Any Language

### People

From these accounts

To these accounts

Mentioning these accounts

### Places

Near this place — Cheltenham, England

### Dates

From this date — to

### Other

Select: ☐ Positive :) ☐ Negative :( ☐ Question ? ☐ Include retweets

**Search**

*Figure 4.5. Twitter Advanced Search.*

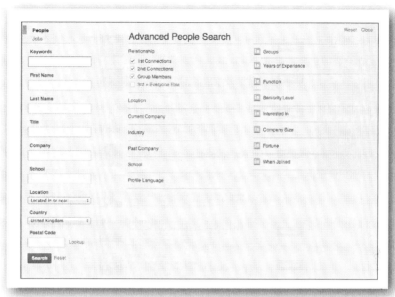

*Figure 4.6. LinkedIn Advanced Search.*

All the social media platforms have their own search facility, which you can use to find users to follow. In particular, Twitter (Figure 4.5) and LinkedIn (Figure 4.6) have highly useful advanced search options that many people are unaware of.

## CASE STUDY

Here's an example of using LinkedIn Advanced Search: I was involved in organising a business event to visit a company who supplied products to the aviation industry. We used LinkedIn Advanced Search to identify prospects who worked in a marketing role, who worked in the aviation/aerospace industry, and who were located within 25 miles of the venue. We reviewed the search results and reached out to people on a one-by-one basis, using social media as a tool for a traditional direct marketing approach. The message was simple – 'I'd like to introduce myself … I found your details through an advanced search on LinkedIn, and I thought you would be interested in an event that's coming up.' We filled all the spaces at that event, and many people have returned to attend other similar events.

LinkedIn's Advanced Search has the added benefit of being able to save searches. Once your search is set, you can receive daily or weekly alerts (via email) of any profiles that are created/updated to match your criteria.

*Figure 4.7. Followerwonk, a Moz app, is a useful Twitter analytics tool. Image used with permission from Moz.*

One of my favourite social media tools, Followerwonk (see Figure 4.7), allows users to find Twitter accounts by searching bios for keywords, and by location. It can be a useful alternative to the native advanced search within Twitter.

## Competitors

If you're looking for your target audience, chances are they might already be following and engaging with your competitors. This makes it easy – go to competitor profiles and work your way through, following their followers (but only if they match your target audience profile). Sounds time-consuming, but Followerwonk can help here too. You can compare Twitter accounts to find overlaps and new audiences, analyse accounts they follow, and see who is following them. Take a look and see what opportunities you can find – the free version provides plenty of information, though you might wish to upgrade for unlimited searches and report downloads.

These are just some of the ways to find your audiences on social media – your specific circumstances and strategy will at some stage guide you to other areas. In Chapter 6 we will look at content of interest to them. In Chapter 7 we will discuss how to evaluate the success of social media activity, which is very much underpinned by having a clearly defined target audience.

## Stay front-of-mind

It's human nature to rank things. People remember firsts – the first person to walk on the moon, the first person to climb Mount Everest. It's therefore key for you and your product or service to rank first in the minds of your target audience.

Positioning is a marketing term, identified by Ries and Trout over 30 years ago, for creating the perception of a product, brand or company identity. Ries and Trout say 'positioning is not what you do to a product. Positioning is what you do to the mind of the prospect. That is, you position (place) the product in the mind of the prospect.' And so marketers have a task to create an image or identity for products, brands and companies. To be successful, Ries and Trout say, you need to connect with what is in your prospect's mind. You need to stay active and in front of your audience, ready for recall when the time is right. Social media is an excellent tool for this.

## Relax!

- The key to getting results on social media is to have an in-depth understanding of your target audience. A good way to do this is to create personas.

- It might be a good idea to revisit your social media profiles. In Chapter 3 we focused on making a good first impression – is that aligned with the needs of your target audience and their preferred social media platforms?
- Your business will have multiple target audiences. Those you might need to consider include:
  - current customers
  - potential customers
  - media (e.g. journalists)
  - suppliers
  - influencers.
- Finding your audience on social media requires research, but there are plenty of tools to help, including native advanced search, and third-party applications such as Followerwonk.

# CHAPTER 5

## Mastering the art of listening

© Clarketoons.com

Listening gives you the opportunity to gain a business advantage. Insight into what your customers, competitors and peers are thinking, saying and doing can provide valuable direction to marketing, product development, customer service and recruitment activities. The ultimate aim of social media listening is to discover all the content relevant to an organisation, brand or issue in a timely fashion. In this chapter, you will learn how to master the art of listening.

> Most people do not listen with the intent to
> understand; they listen with the intent to reply.
> STEPHEN R. COVEY

This quote is, I believe, one of the most powerful I have ever come across. Habit 5 in Covey's *The 7 Habits of Highly Effective People* focuses on principles of empathic communication: that is, 'seek first to understand, then to be understood.'

Covey explains that, in the communications industry, we rarely diagnose before we prescribe. We dive straight in with answers and have a tendency to filter what we hear through our own paradigms, reading our own autobiography into other people's lives. We answer with what *we* would do, but that isn't always likely to be the correct answer. We often don't put ourselves in other people's shoes.

Empathic listening means listening with the intent to understand, to get inside another person's frame of reference or worldview. We mentioned using one-to-one or group interviews to prepare personas, and these are highly valid, but only represent a snapshot in time. They are also limited to how people respond when questioned: real-life behaviour can sometimes differ.

In Chapter 3 we introduced keywords, and their importance in getting you and your business found online. In Chapter 4 we learnt how they can help us build an audience. Social media listening tools are also keyword-based, so it's again important to understand what terms people might use when talking about your business and its wider context.

When you truly understand your audience, you can focus on problem-solving: that is, showing how you can help your audience overcome their challenges and achieve their goals with your product or service. Covey explains: 'Because you really listen, you become influenceable. And being influenceable is the key to influencing others.' It's the key to getting your message heard and shared, to gaining trust and doing business.

## Social media listening

Social media listening is the process of identifying and assessing what is being said about a company, individual, product or brand on the internet, and the issues that affect it. Social media listening supports all objectives, from marketing to HR and customer service.

'Now that people are plugged in, they are rarely disconnected – and the result is a constant channel of thoughts and opinions from the brain directly to the screen. This is the era of what I call consumer-generated media, or CGM,' says Paul Blackshaw, author of *Satisfied Customers Tell Three Friends, Angry Customers Tell 3,000: Running a Business in Today's Consumer-Driven World*.

He goes on: 'CGM is the currency of a new commercial relationship between business and consumers. It is the endless stream of comments, opinions, emotions and personal stories about any and every company, product, service, or brand, which consumers can now post online and broadcast to millions of other consumers with the click of a mouse … CGM is the true barometer of corporate and brand credibility.'

Every day, 24/7, consumers are posting content and starting conversations about customer service issues, their intent to purchase, and providing product feedback. If you are listening, these are all valuable opportunities – to steer engaged prospects towards sales, to turn brand advocates into evangelists, and to manage potential crises. Social media listening helps you to understand pain points, to validate audience personas, to shape content plans and to provide market intelligence. It also helps you to be the first to respond; SAVO Group (savogroup.com) suggest that 74% of prospects choose to buy from the company that was first to help them along their buyer's journey.

How great would it be to post on Twitter that you're in a certain location, hungry and not sure where to go to eat? If a company is listening to that search query, they could quickly respond; perhaps even offer you a discount voucher!

Think about which search queries you could be monitoring for your product or service.

# Start with why

In Chapter 2 we discovered Simon Sinek's 'Golden Circle' concept that focuses on *why* we do what we do. If you missed it, take a look at it now. A social media listening programme must start with knowing *why* you are listening. This means, of course, understanding your business strategy and marketing goals. Only then can you determine what you really need to listen out for.

You may want to:

- monitor the success of a press release or product/service promotion;
- track what is being said about your company and products, both positive and negative;
- conduct competitor or market research; or
- monitor infringement of trademark or other intellectual property.

Stephen Rappaport, author of *Listen First! Turning Social Media Conversations Into Business Advantage*, highlights two types of online listening, each of which has a unique purpose:

- **Social monitoring**: tracking online brand mentions on a daily basis for public relations, brand protection, operations and customer outreach and engagement. Social monitoring is continuous, to enable reporting on conversation volume and to respond to events.
- **Social research**: analysing naturally occurring online categories of conversation to better understand why people do what they do, the role of brands in their lives, and the product, branding and communications implications for brand owners. Social research is strategic, ad hoc, and used for campaign planning, new product/service development, or improving the online experience.

## How to listen

Tools for social media listening vary from one-off advanced searching within the social media platforms, as we saw in Chapter 4, to daily or weekly feeds of simple keyword monitoring via **Google Alerts**, to sophisticated tools such as **Radian6**, **MeltwaterBuzz** or **Brandwatch** which monitor quite complex search queries and provide sentiment analysis. Brandwatch define sentiment analysis as 'the process of determining the emotional tone bethind a series of words, used to gain an understanding of the attitudes, opinions and emotions expressed within an online mention.' Some tools are freely available, while others attract a monthly or annual subscription fee. A summary of useful tools can be found in the resource section at the end of this book. Both ends of the spectrum provide invaluable audience, industry and competitor insight and opportunity information.

## *Google Alerts*

If you're not already using Google Alerts, get going now (visit google. co.uk/alerts) – it takes just a few minutes to set up. By creating a Google Alert, you can receive a notification any time Google finds new results on topics that interest you. You could set up a Google Alert for your own name, your business name, your brand name, competitors, keywords, etc. The more precise the search terms for your alerts are, the more relevant your notifications will be. It's a great way to keep up with information online, it's fun and it's free.

## *Twitter lists*

If you are using Twitter, make sure you create some lists. A Twitter list is a curated group of Twitter accounts; they can be a great way to manage your listening activity. Content curation (selecting and organising relevant information) is an important aspect of content marketing, as we will discover in Chapter 6. Twitter lists can be public or private; you can create your own lists or subscribe to lists created by others. For example, I have specific lists for local media contacts, key resources, event attendees, etc. You do not need to be following accounts that are in a Twitter list, which makes them a great way to (a) follow competitors without them knowing, and (b) keep your follower:following ratio in check (more on this later in the Chapter). There is also a great tool called **If This Then That** (ifttt.com) which can automate list-building – for example, anyone mentioning a specific hashtag can be added to a Twitter list.

## Social media listening – for customer service

As consumers, we have high expectations from companies, particularly around customer service. Businesses lose staggering amounts of money, customers and goodwill due to poor customer service – and consumers will post online if they are unhappy with the service they receive.

Customer service complaints online are highly visible, which in part is why company Facebook or Twitter pages have become go-to places for getting a swift response. Fast response times and effective handling of customer service issues can reflect well on an organisation.

As mentioned in Chapter 3, it helps to manage expectations by including service hours in a social media account bio. Many well-run social media accounts also post this information regularly. Some even publish expected response times – how great is that for customer service management?

Social customer service includes listening for complaints, compliments and support requests, including problems and questions. When listening, it can be useful to set up monitoring and follow up processes around:

- **who** has posted (customer, prospect, media)
- **what** category of post it is (complaint, feedback, advocacy)
- **what** the underlying customer emotion is (anger, frustration, hurt).

Consider having predefined messages and rehearse these as part of the training process. Responses can take place both publicly and/or privately, via direct messaging. It is important to acknowledge the query publicly and to manage expectations for a more detailed response, which may or may not take place online.

It's also interesting to note that many organisations running social customer service programmes are saving money: using social media not only costs less than telephone and email communications, but it can also resolve matters much more quickly. Listening is a great way to transform a negative into a positive; a problem into an opportunity; customers into advocates. There are many award-winning case studies that detail such activity (see the links in the resource section at the end of the book).

# Reputation management

> Your most unhappy customers are your
> greatest source of learning.
> BILL GATES

The attention we earn by being active on social media is, on the whole, positive. However, there are occasions when user-generated messages can adversely affect customers' perception of your business and cause reputational damage. If there are potential issues that you don't wish you or your business to be associated with – for example, environmental damage or vulnerable persons – then you should set up and monitor these as specific subjects to listen out for.

CASE STUDY

Occasionally I use social media to highlight poor customer service – in part to ease my frustration, and in part to get a case study! I'm often impressed by a company's swift response and resolution (which restores my faith in the company). More impressive is when a competing company reaches out to see if they can help me instead. I did, however, have one unexpected outcome to a complaint I made on Twitter. The company I had cause to complain about was clearly listening to mentions of their brand, but instead of responding directly to me (publicly or privately) with a message, they blocked me from viewing their Twitter account! A case study of 'what not to do'.

## How to manage a crisis on social media

In times of crisis, information is power – organisations must be listening and ready to respond to comments as quickly (and as accurately) as possible. Crises are highly prevalent in the travel industry, where incidents and delays affect large numbers of people. We love to talk about the weather in the UK, and inevitably adverse weather conditions cause travel crises.

Textbook crisis communications suggest a pattern of responses that starts with: 'We're aware of the situation. We're looking into it. We'll share more information as soon as we have it.' Updates can then be posted as appropriate.

After identifying an issue, it's time to evaluate the situation, and a 'triage' system can work well to prioritise responses and determine whether or not there is a need to escalate. A number of factors may be considered here. For example:

- **what** is being said – the seriousness of the issue (rank on a scale from 1 to 10);
- **who** is saying it – the influence or authority of the person who posts it (this can have a knock-on effect on others' perceptions of the issue);
- **frequency** – is the issue getting more visible, or less? How many times are you being mentioned?

Priority should clearly be given to the most serious of issues and those who have great influence should be managed most carefully.

There are few reputational crises that you can't predict or prepare for as part of your business strategy and planning activity – consult your PR and communications team or work with an external consultant to assess your risk and create a traffic light monitoring system. Scenario planning and likely responses should always be included in a social media policy and staff training (see 'managing risk' in Chapter 8). It's important to recognise that criticism should not be ignored. Criticism represents valuable insight, and can be turned into a positive – if managed well. Such comments should not be deleted, but the comment needs to be acknowledged as quickly as possible and taken offline – into the real world.

## Social selling

Social selling is when a salesperson uses social media to engage and interact with prospects and customers. Part of the process is to provide a good first impression, to demonstrate knowledge and credibility, and build trust. Another part requires data gathering. As part of the social selling process, listening tools can be used to:

- find discussions/questions about your product category
- find intent-to-purchase signals
- look for recommendation requests within your product category
- monitor target prospect personas to confirm accuracy
- discover relevant content to share (and demonstrate expertise).

Mining social media platforms for information like this can be of huge assistance to sales professionals. As Covey says in *The 7 Habits of Highly Effective People*, the amateur salesperson 'sells products; the professional sells solutions to needs and problems.' Listening and responding with relevant, helpful information is a great way to start a relationship, and means the selling is not too overt or pushy. It's a great support and complement to traditional sales activity.

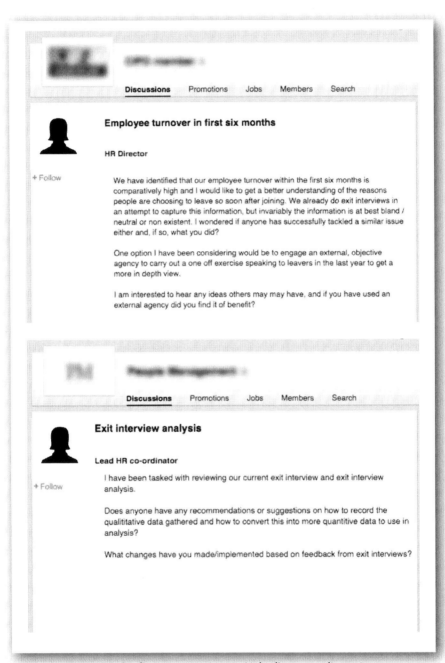

Figure 5.1. Finding opportunities in LinkedIn group discussions.

*Figure 5.2. Twilert sends you email alerts of Tweets containing your keywords.
Image used with permission from Twilert.*

## CASE STUDY

In early 2015 I worked with a client who provided bespoke
research software for human resources. We were looking
for ways to identify new business opportunities. As part
of the project, we spent time identifying relevant LinkedIn
groups – groups in which HR professionals were engaging in
discussions. From a long list of potential groups, we refined
the list to four or five key groups that seemed to be the right
membership profile and showed active discussions about
industry issues. We observed the conversations, searched the
group, and found our gold (see Figure 5.1). We did not dive
straight in with a sales message. We watched the comments
appear. We took note of the challenges and the feedback.
We crafted our response and, on an individual basis, made
contact (outside LinkedIn), personally addressing the issue,
how we had heard of their need, and listing how we could
help. One LinkedIn group discussion provided my client with
enough business opportunities for the next 12 months.

A very easy tool to use for real-time alerts is **Twilert** (twilert.com; see Figure 5.2). It's similar to the Google Alerts mentioned earlier. Not only can Twilert listen on your behalf and send you emails whenever your keywords, brand names or hashtags are mentioned, but it helps you to find leads that are relevant to your business through a combination of geolocation, language and keyword searches. Businesses can quickly benefit from receiving notifications whenever someone asks for a recommendation related to their product or service in their area.

## A note about influencers

With social media has come a shift in trust. We not only ask our family, friends and colleagues for opinion, but we also look at reviews such as those on Amazon and TripAdvisor and make purchases (business and personal) based on recommendations and ratings from strangers. It's interesting how even people we don't know can have an influence on our behaviour – would you book a hotel that had poor TripAdvisor ratings, or buy a book from Amazon that had several one-star reviews?

Influencer marketing is emerging as a new marketing trend, in which a focus is placed on key individuals rather than the target market as a whole. Like strangers on review sites, influencers can shape purchasing decisions without ever being accountable for them.

If you recall the different types of social media user (see Chapter 2), then you will recall that some users can be highly influential – for example, the 'cliquers' in their small network, or the 'sparks', who are the most active and deeply engaged users of social media platforms. But how do we find these users? Sometimes it is easy – press, industry analysts, business reports, etc. Some are less easy to identify, and so the answer is social media listening. For example, you may notice a small number of users regularly using the keywords (hashtags) you are monitoring. You might also notice the same users appearing in your Google Alerts. You can also go in search of influencers, using tools such as **Klout** or **Kred**. (Klout.com and kred.com are websites that use social media analytics to rank its users according to online social influence, which is a numerical value between 1 and 100).

While they are useful tools, Klout and Kred only provide a number, and a little more information is useful when assessing possible influencers to work with. Here are some more questions to consider:

- Do they have large networks of people that engage with them?
- Who are their followers/connections? (i.e. do they keep good company?)
- How often do they post content?
- What are the key topics of the content they share?
- Are people sharing/engaging with their content?
- On Twitter, do they have a credible following:follower ratio? (The higher the ratio in favour of followers, the more influential the Tweeter.)

Most importantly, make sure you choose influencers who are relevant to you, your business and your target audience. Remember also that each social media platform is different, and there may be several influencers sharing opinions across the platforms.

## Relax!

- Before you do anything else with social media, plan a programme for listening and responding to mentions of your brand.
- Set up Google Alerts and Twitter lists for simple keyword listening.
- You may begin by listening for:
  - your company name
  - names of key executives and employees
  - product names
  - competitors' names (company name and key executives)
  - industry-specific keywords.
- Be prepared for reputation management and potential crisis management by planning responses in advance. Create a traffic light system for monitoring.
- Identify and build relationships with possible influencers who can help increase awareness and generate opportunities for you and your business.

# CHAPTER 6

# Content marketing and storytelling

The era of mass marketing has gone. We used to shout loudly and repeatedly at people to get attention. We used to send out large-volume direct marketing campaigns to as many people as possible, hoping that a small percentage would respond. Thankfully, advertisers have now learnt that less is more, and a considered use of data and targeting can leverage the same, if not better, results. Good marketers have focused their efforts on being in the right place, at the right time, with the right message. It's all about content: words, knowledge and information.

> Content marketing is all the marketing that's left.
> SETH GODIN

In Chapter 5 we focused on the art of listening, but the focus of this chapter is on how to start delivering information. As Stephen R. Covey said: 'Seek first to understand, then to be understood.'

American author and entrepreneur Seth Godin is one of my marketing heroes. I had the great fortune to meet him in 2015 at a live five-hour Q&A event at Imperial College, London. He talks a lot about the way ideas spread. What Godin meant by 'content marketing is all the marketing that's left' is that we should only be creating content that our audience cares about: content that they want to read, watch and/or listen to. He confirms that the old way of marketing saw customers constantly being interrupted with one-way messages. He believes that new marketing is about connecting with customers: it's about telling authentic stories, teaching customers, and giving customers the resources to know, like and trust us. And, if we prepare good content, which solves customers' problems, it will be talked about and shared.

If this is all true, which I believe it is, then the marketing challenge is hugely overwhelming. However, if we understand our objectives, and create a plan, we can achieve success.

Let's break it down.

## What is content marketing?

According to the Content Marketing Institute (CMI), 'Content marketing is a strategic marketing approach focused on creating and distributing valuable, relevant and consistent content to attract and retain a clearly defined audience – and ultimately, drive profitable customer action'.

The term 'content marketing' has been around for a while, and goes hand in hand with the rise in social media use. Again, it's what we've always done – it just seems have gained popularity and become a new buzzword. Social media has given individuals, and businesses, the opportunity not just to consume online content, but also to publish their own content to a potentially worldwide audience.

The CMI summarises the concept as follows: 'Basically, content marketing is the art of communicating with your customers and prospects without selling. It is non-interruption marketing. Instead of pitching your products or services, you are delivering information that makes your buyer more intelligent … If we, as businesses, deliver consistent, ongoing valuable information to buyers, they ultimately reward us with their business and loyalty'.

So, how do we do this?

## The content marketing process

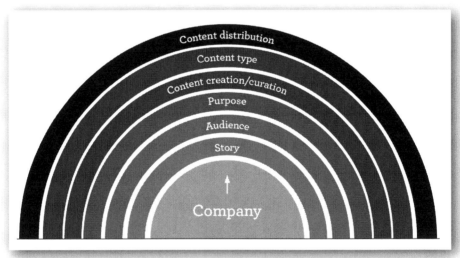

*Figure 6.1. The content marketing planning process.*

When researching this book I was amazed that I could not find a clear end-to-end explanation for how to plan content marketing. I could find plenty of 'how to's' and plenty of fear-inducing 'It's so complicated that it all needs to be outsourced because you'll never have the time to do it properly' type articles. I hope that Figure 6.1 and the journey this book is taking you on are helping you to feel that it *can* be done, if you have a plan.

Let's look at Figure 6.1 in more detail, taking each band in turn.

## 1. Company

Remember the TED talk we mentioned in Chapter 2? In it, Sinek said that the 'why' of your company is the core of how you should be communicating. Any marketing activity, including content marketing, must start with understanding your company's business strategy. If the plan requires tactical use of social media to achieve its objectives, this will require content. (Note, just as in the discussion in Chapter 2 about social media not being a strategy, *content marketing, in itself, is* not a *strategy*.)

## 2. Story

> Marketing is no longer about the stuff you sell, but about the stories you tell.
> SETH GODIN

From prehistoric cave paintings to big-budget Hollywood movies, the desire to tell and hear stories is an important part of the human experience, and a valuable way to remember sequences of events. As children, we learn through stories. A story gives people a reason to sympathise with characters, to care about what they are saying, and to understand a plot. Stories are shared, they create a following, and the best ones inspire audiences to act and believe.

And as adults in business, we each have our own professional story. To be known as a credible, authentic source of information and to gain others' trust, we need to define and tell our story in a focused, consistent way. So, how do we go about telling stories in business?

Answer: We prepare key messages.
A good framework for developing key messages is 'Message, Support, Action'.

- **Message**: What do you need your audience to know about you and your business?
- **Support**: What information or facts do you have to support the message? You should have up to three pieces of supporting evidence for each key message.
- **Action**: Is there a call to action? What should someone do in response to the message?

> People don't buy what you do, they buy why you do it.
> SIMON SINEK

Remember the 'Golden Circle', and focus on the 'why', not just the 'how' and 'what'. Tell people what they can do with your product, not what the product does. Let them know what problem you solved, and why that was a real problem. Share testimonials to demonstrate how your customers felt after experiencing your service. Appeal to people's rational and emotional senses. We all have hearts as well as minds, even when we're doing business.

Here is an example of my own key messages:

| Message | Support | Action |
|---------|---------|--------|
| I believe that good marketing can help a business grow. I can advise business owners on how to make their business grow. | I was marketing manager for a B2B marketing services organisation that saw high growth: from £3 million to £60 million over five years.

I have examples of my work and testimonials from the managing director and other colleagues.

I can also name other clients I have worked with, who had similar requirements, and share with you details of how I have helped them too. | Get in touch; let's have a meeting. |

Develop four or five key messages, write them down and refer to them regularly. Do not change these key messages, unless there is a big change in your strategy. These are top-level messages about the core of your business that should apply to all audiences. You might find that the supporting information can be updated, but the messaging itself should not fundamentally change. This process can apply to individuals building a personal brand as well as for businesses.

The more often these key messages are communicated, the more they will be heard and understood. If you want to read more about making ideas 'sticky', check out *Made to Stick* by Chip and Dan Heath. They take a look at why some ideas take hold and others come unstuck, pinpointing six factors that reveal how our minds absorb information and what we can do to make sure our own ideas register with others. As well as *simplicity*, *unexpectedness*, *concreteness*, *credibility* and *emotion*, Heath and Heath highlight the importance of *stories* and their power to stimulate and expire. (I highly recommend this book – it's listed in the resource section at the end of this book.)

And so, your key messages become a checklist for every piece of content you produce, and every communication opportunity that arises. If it's not on your checklist, then don't pursue it. Stay true to your story.

CASE STUDY

For example, I received a telephone call from a journalist asking if I would like to offer an expert commentary on the latest John Lewis Christmas advertisement. As much as I would have loved to have my name in a national press article, I declined the opportunity. Why? Because it didn't fit with my key messages.

## 3. Audience

> Content marketing is about delivering the
> content your audience is seeking in all
> the places they are searching for it.
> MICHAEL BRENNER

If you recall the target audience personas discussed in Chapter 4, it should be starting to become clear that the stories we tell need to solve the problems faced by our audience, and include information about the solution your business can provide. For example, the retailer Long Tall Sally provides clothing for tall women. They solve #tallgirlproblems. Insight gained from social media listening (see Chapter 5) can be used to add detail to these challenges.

Although we have discussed defining a target customer, we have not yet discussed the journey they take to becoming a customer. We know what our customers might look like, but they might not yet be aware that

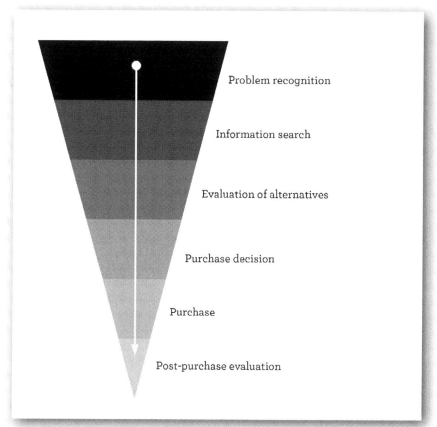

Figure 6.2. The consumer buying decision process (Engel, Blackwell and Kollat, 1968).

we even exist! Further, potential customers might not make themselves known to us immediately – customers carry out a great deal of research, often online, before they make contact with a company. This means we need to have expert content ready for them to find and to answer their questions, and encourage them to make contact with us. The aim of putting content out there is to create a conversation with your target audience.

Whether it's a B2C or B2B product or service, consumers all go through a buying decision process (see Figure 6.2). Depending on the product or service, the timescale for the process may differ. The decision to buy a pair of shoes, for example, is made much more quickly than a decision about which accounting software to invest in.

The process begins with problem recognition. This may not always be triggered by the customer; it might be stimulated by some content you share about your product or service, helping the potential customer realise that they have a need that should be solved.

Once a problem is recognised, the information search process begins. Potential customers are looking for recommendations and trusted advisors. The research process continues and customers begin to evaluate alternatives; testimonials and case studies that offer reassurance are key at this stage. Then it's time for the purchase decision – and you need to stay close to that prospective customer, offering reminders that you are the right solution to solve their problem. After purchase, the process has not ended. The customer must decide whether or not they are satisfied with the decision they have made, and if they'll recommend your product or service to others.

## 4. Purpose

If content is there to help your business to move a potential customer through the buying process, then the purpose of each piece of content produced must match the customer's needs at each stage.

Sonja Jefferson and Sharon Tanton, authors of *Valuable Content Marketing*, offer a quality control guide to help ensure content works for clients, customers and businesses. They say valuable content is:

- '*useful* – it educates, informs or entertains
- *focused* – it is relevant and meaningful to its target audience
- *clear and compelling* – it tells a story that people understand and respond to

- *high quality* – it is interesting, well produced, with substance
- *genuine* – it is written from the heart by people who care.'

At this stage of defining the purpose of our content, we should be focusing on our objectives. We should also be ensuring that 'relevancy' is at the heart of everything we are doing. I think the illustration below makes this very clear.

© Clarketoons.com

• • •

Remember how, at the start of the chapter, we looked at how marketing had changed from broadcasting to customers to engagement with customers? Content needs to be engaging to move potential customers through the buying decision process.

Think of a radio station playing in the background at a party. A few people may be paying attention to it, and a few more may not be paying attention but still realise it's on, but the majority, however, don't hear it at all. The radio is simply broadcasting.

A live DJ arrives. He's also there to play music, but every so often the DJ calls a guest by name and asks them what they would like to hear. The guest responds and the DJ plays the request. He does the same again a bit later on. The DJ is engaging with his audience.

Imagine doing the same with your content: finding your audience (or making it easy for them to find you, and join your party), inspiring them with content so that they become *aware* of you and develop an *interest* in finding out more about you. This is the perfect time in social media for making connections, liking, following, and so on.

Next comes the *desire* to find out more about working together, whether that's arranging a meeting, putting together a proposal or arranging a trial. We're moving along that journey to achieving an objective. The final step will be *action*. Yes, it's that AIDA communications model we introduced in Chapter 2 (did you spot it?)

The dictionary definition of engagement is 'to occupy or attract someone's interest or attention; involve someone in a conversation or discussion'. More simply, it means getting your audience to do something in response to your content. When you actively engage with individuals and companies, there's a greater chance that they will reciprocate.

The power of content lies in its potential to start a conversation: to encourage people to engage with you and your business. Engagement is a function of trust and knowledge, and takes time to build. To get results with social media, you can't just broadcast content hoping your audience will pay attention and respond (because they won't). To get results, you've first got to focus on engagement.

Engagement means slightly different things on different social media platforms, and we'll see in Chapter 7 how engagement is an important measurement of social media activity. For the tools we have been focusing on in this book, it means:

- LinkedIn – likes, comments, shares, views
- Twitter – replies, mentions, Retweets, likes
- Facebook – likes, comments, shares
- Instagram – likes, comments, shares
- Google+ - comments, favourites, shares, likes (+1).

Does the content you're posting encourage engagement? Do you have content that matches the needs of your target audience/s at each stage of the buying decision process? Is the content valuable i.e. useful, focused, clear and compelling, high quality and genuine?

If the answer is no, it's OK. We can fix it. Let's take a look at content creation/curation.

## 5. Content creation/curation

'Finding the time' and 'creating original content' are often cited as the biggest social media challenges.

A simple rule related to content is the 'rule of thirds', which ensures that you have a good mix of topics. The three areas are:

1. Promoting yourself, and your business
2. Recommending interesting stuff: 'how to' articles, industry research, latest trends
3. Letting us get to know you: tell us interesting things about what you're doing (but keep it focused on your business strategy and objectives).

Not only are we now all content publishers, but we are all editors: receiving news and information, and making decisions on what to share with our audiences. But, we don't need to *create* all of the content that we deliver. It's important to share content from other social media users too.

The content you share should always align with your key messages. Focus on sharing content that your target audience will be interested in, and content that supports what you want to be known for. Don't forget to give credit to the content's creator and the site where it originated.

I find the most effective way to curate content is via RSS (Rich Site Summary or Really Simple Syndication). Many news-related sites, blogs and other online publishers syndicate their content as an RSS feed. To keep up to date with this content you'll need an RSS reader. I use **Feedly** (feedly.com) as it's a great way to collect content from a variety of sources, including RSS. It's worth spending time seeking out relevant content on the web to add to your reader; I find industry press a great place to start. We mentioned Google Alerts in Chapter 5; I also have these delivered to Feedly. A news aggregator such as Feedly can save you time, as you don't need to visit each site individually. It also helps to reduce inbox clutter as you don't need to sign up for each site's email newsletter. I organise my content into subject categories and check it out once or twice a day over a cup of coffee. From Feedly I can schedule and share content directly to my social media profiles (I use a Google Chrome extension for **Hootsuite**, my preferred social media management tool. More on Hootsuite in Chapter 8).

In Chapter 4 we looked at hashtags as a way to search for people. You can also use them to find relevant content to share! Trending topics and their hashtags can also be identified on your Twitter.com homepage – a useful way to find 'in the moment' conversations to get involved in – but only if you can match the opportunity to your messaging grid. There have been some classic cases of successful 'newsjacking' on social media – such as Oreo's 'Power out? No problem. You can still dunk in the dark' Tweet, which was posted during the 2013 SuperBowl. However, there are also examples of the inappropriate use of events to promote a brand, from extreme weather to celebrity deaths, and this should – obviously – be avoided.

We also mentioned Twitter lists in Chapter 5 – they are a perfect way to manage a list of accounts that post content you might wish to share with your own audience (I have created a Twitter list specifically for this).

When sharing curated content, it is important to add your own commentary to give context to it, and to show you're not just blindly sharing posts – it doesn't need to be a long explanation, just enough to let people know your intention and reason for sharing. As a minimum, original authors should be tagged in curated content. This is likely to create a 'thank you' response. Similarly, anyone who shares your content with a mention should be thanked. This is engagement!

## 6. Content type

Once you know your 'why' and 'what' (purpose), you need to decide how to present your content by considering which types and formats will be most appropriate for you, your message, your target customer (remember our personas should include information about communication preferences), and where they are in the buying decision process.

We can break down content into four different types:

- **written form**: for example, blogs, white papers, guides, checklists, reports, presentations, e-books and books
- **visual**: for example, product imagery, team photography and infographics
- **audio and video**: for example, event coverage, demonstrations and interviews, webinars and podcasts
- **interactive**: for example, quizzes, calculators, polls, games and competitions.

These are either:

- user-focused – for example, customer testimonials, endorsements, reviews and ratings
  or
- product-focused – for example, 'how to' guides, fact sheets, checklists, Q&As/FAQs.

In the early stages of the buying decision process an infographic or video might be more appropriate to the information-gathering needs of your target audience. Longer form, written content, such as white papers and e-books, are most likely to be read further down the buying decision process, when a greater depth of information is required. Whatever content you produce, quality is more important than quantity. You don't want to overload your audience with information, or they will switch off.

Social media status updates could include any of these format types, depending on the platform. They can also be used in combination. For example, Instagram updates will be visual, supported by a short descriptor and keywords (hashtags). A LinkedIn, Twitter, Facebook or Google+ short-form written update might be supported by an image, a link to a long-form written blog, or a video.

And it's OK to give away information for free. There is real value in being helpful in order to build trust and long-term relationships. If you wish, ask for an exchange of information before providing content – such as asking for contact details – but don't worry about giving too much knowledge away for free. Remember, people buy your 'why', and not the 'how' or 'what' information contained in your content. What you do is not your unique selling point; you are selling how you add value to what you do. In turn, more people will want to work with you and your existing customers will want to keep their business with you.

Finally, you should also consider how your content might be consumed – for example, on a mobile, tablet or desktop.

## CASE STUDY

Your own data might help you determine how your content is consumed.

For example, in examining Google Analytics for a local estate agent's website, the data revealed that most visitors used a mobile or tablet. However, visitors using a desktop computer spent more time on the site and they submitted more details via desktop, suggesting that the customer journey starts on mobile, when they become aware of the estate agent and the properties they have available, but shifts to desktop when the information-gathering becomes more detailed. Content types could be adapted according to the stage of decision making.

For an office supplies company, Google Analytics data revealed that on the first website visit a user was highly focused on obtaining a product brochure. A returning visitor spent more time on the website, looking at other areas such as 'about the team' and 'service FAQs'. The buying decision process was very easy to identify and content could be tailored to the different stages and different information needs of the target audience.

Now, it's time for the final stage of the content planning process...

## 7. Content distribution

> 'Build it, and they will come' only works in the movies. Social media is a 'build it, nurture it, engage them and they may come and stay'.
> SETH GODIN

We have two clear goals for our content:

1) to be seen and be found – by the right people, at the right time (in the buying decision process), and
2) to maximise its shelf life.

## Paid, earned, owned and shared distribution

There are four types of media for distributing content. Traditionally, marketers only had to worry about paid and earned media, but with social media came the opportunity for owned and shared media.

- **Paid media** is what we know of as advertising: traditionally, space in a newspaper or magazine, on radio, television, etc. Today businesses spend more money online, either with Google, social media platforms themselves or with third parties who will distribute content on your behalf.

Opportunities exist for a variety of content types, from sponsored links to white paper libraries.

- **Earned media** is what we might know as media relations. Traditionally this was all about journalists, but today can include online influencers, including bloggers and vloggers (video bloggers). Although earned media is hard to control, an independent endorsement of your business is highly credible.
- **Owned media** is your own content, hosted on your own platform – for example, your website. This is arguably the most important of all media, as it's within your control. Don't forget that driving traffic to your website is likely to be a key objective for social media activity.
- **Shared media:** in Chapter 2 we looked at the honeycomb of social media and identified sharing as one of its seven building blocks. Whether it's LinkedIn, Twitter, Facebook, Instagram, Google+ or any other social media platform, this is where content is shared and where conversations begin.

Unless a content piece has a need (and fit) to be highly topical, a good piece of content should be 'evergreen'. After all your effort in planning and creating content, you don't want it to be a one-hit wonder. The lifespan of any post on social media is just a few hours, so don't forget to repeat your messages (see 'best times to post content on social media', below).

Most content produced within your business can also be repurposed into different formats for sharing across social media platforms. For example, you can create an infographic from the key headlines in a research report. The infographic can be posted on Twitter and Facebook, with a link to a website landing page (for the full report to be downloaded). A report could also be formatted into presentation format and posted on **Slideshare** (a platform owned by LinkedIn), which attracts its own visitors and drives website traffic. Slideshare presentations are regularly embedded into LinkedIn profiles.

Think about your existing content and how you might repurpose and distribute it across different social media platforms and other marketing channels.

## A content marketing plan

Now, it's time to gather all this detail into a plan. During the planning process I find I use a lot of sticky notes! Write down anything and everything – don't judge your ideas until you have finished.

© Clarketoons.com

For each content idea, ensure you note down:

- which of your key messages it relates to (if it doesn't fit, throw that idea away)
- which audience persona it is targeted towards
- what stage of the buying decision process the idea supports
- which keywords (hashtags) to use within the content and when distributing the content
- what content type is most suitable
- how you will distribute the content – paid, owned, earned and/ or shared.

Then, group your ideas into a calendar. Decide if any ideas are timing-specific and fix those into the calendar. Decide on your approach for everything else, keeping in mind your available resources for creating and curating – it's far better to produce less content, of higher quality, than it is to produce high volumes of lower-quality content.

For example, you might decide to have an editorial plan that includes:

- daily – 3 Tweets, 2 Facebook posts, 2 Instagram posts
- weekly – 1 blog, 1 LinkedIn group discussion, 2 LinkedIn status updates, 3 Google+ posts
- monthly – podcast, case study
- quarterly – white paper, webinar.

You can find a template editorial calendar on my website, luanwise.co.uk/how-i-help

## The best time to post content on social media

| Social Media Platform | Time | Day | Frequency |
|---|---|---|---|
| LinkedIn | | M T W T T S S | 2-5 posts per week |
| Twitter | | M T W T F S S | 3+ posts per day |
| Facebook | | M T W T F S S | 2 posts per day |
| Instagram | | M T W T T S S | 2 posts per day |
| Google+ | | M T W T T S S | 3-5 posts per week |

Figure 6.3. The best time to post content on social media.

A question I hear all the time is 'What are the best times to post on social media?' The answer is, it depends! It depends on the platform, your audience and your objectives.

Your strategic objective will never be 'to post five times a day on Twitter'. The number-one rule is to *only post when you have something relevant to say.*

You will find that certain days of the week and times of day provide more engagement than others. Posting content when your audience is online and ready to respond is key. Consider that LinkedIn is a business-to-business networking platform so users are most likely to be online Monday to Friday, 9am to 5pm. I find Facebook use increases around lunchtime and evening. Look at when your competitors are posting. Test different combinations and see what response you receive to each post. Only you can decide the best time and day to post content. Take a look at your website visitors (via Google Analytics) and see if there are patterns you can follow. You could also use a tool such as **Tweriod** to find out the best times to Tweet. Measuring the effectiveness of your social media activity is discussed in Chapter 7.

Figure 6.3 is a good template to use when planning. There are guidelines for the frequency of posting, which relate more to the pace of each platform. A Tweet will be gone from user timelines in a few hours; a LinkedIn post might last a few days. Again, there are no hard and fast answers, so the checklist above is for guidance and planning only. The correct answer to 'What are the best times to post on social media?' can only be found in your own data.

After a while, you may not need to plan every piece of content in detail, particularly the daily messages; with social media, it's important to stay fluid and act in real time. Social media management tools can be used to schedule evergreen content in advance – as we'll see in Chapter 8 – and then you can focus your daily activity on listening, responding and sharing.

Finally, I suggest pulling together your plan into a one-page summary document that you can constantly refer to. It includes your key messages, and a reminder of your target audience personas, keywords to include (as hashtags), best times to post, what actions you would like your audience to follow, and what you will be measuring. Use this plan as a checklist at all times. The template below (Figure 6.4), along with worked examples, can be found on my website, luanwise.co.uk/how-i-help.

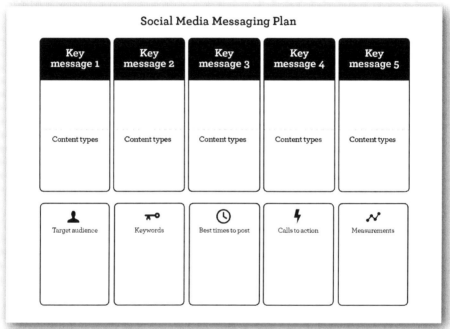

*Figure 6.4. A one-page summary of your plan for using social media.*

## Relax!

- When we're talking about content, we simply mean words, knowledge and information. It's the text we already have in our brochures, on our website, in our credentials documents, etc. We often don't need to create new content specifically for social media.

- Content marketing starts with *why*, and focuses on storytelling. Create your four or five key messages, write them down, and refer to them regularly.
- Audience personas help guide the purpose of social media content – understanding the buyer's decision making process and the need for information at each stage is the key to a successful content marketing plan.
- Content should not be all 'me, me, me'. Great content solves problems for the audience and is their pathway through the buying decision process to purchase your product or service. Remember the 'rule of thirds' and set up alerts/lists/feeds for easy content curation.
- The power of your content lies in its potential to start a conversation. Write with your audience in mind, and focus on engaging your audience.
- Repurposing content for social media ensures each piece has a longer shelf life and can be used across multiple platforms. Due to the fast pace of social media, messages need to be repeated and it's OK to do so. Remember: quality over quantity, engagement over broadcast.

# CHAPTER 7

## Measurements that matter

© Clarketoons.com

Q: What makes a metric meaningful?
A: When you see the metric, do you know what you need to do?

If the answer is 'no', you're probably looking at a vanity metric. The answer needs to be 'yes'! This chapter addresses the mistake of looking at meaningless metrics, and shows you how to focus on the measurements that really matter to you and your business.

Marketing activity has never been easy to measure, and the infamous and frequently quoted statement from US department store merchant Jon Wanamaker – 'Half the money I spend on advertising is wasted; the trouble is, I don't know which half' – rings true.

Social media is simultaneously the most measurable marketing channel, and also the one that is most difficult to assess. Like traditional media, a lot of the added value of social media will never be measurable. There are also a large number of social media users ('onlookers' – see Chapter 2) who are influenced by social media, but who never interact online. Prospects that don't interact with you directly on social media may still be influenced by repeat exposures to your brand and messaging, and may purchase in-store, for example. There is also a need to distinguish between the short-term and long-term effects of social media activity. Activities such as competitions will inevitably result in greater immediate engagement, but they may not provide beneficial long-term effects such as brand loyalty and repeat purchases.

The plethora of social media analytics tools available can also be overwhelming, and although understanding what you are getting back from the time, money and resource you're putting into social media activity is business-critical, the vital factor to bear in mind is that you only need to measure what matters.

All too often, social media measurement is viewed in terms of audience size – by the number of Facebook page likes or Twitter followers. This kind of metric does have its place: for example, it's good to know the size of the opportunity and to aim high in terms of audience acquisition. After all, why stop at 1,000 followers on Twitter if the leading trade magazine in your industry has 40,000? And the size of your audience does matter, because you need an audience in order to have any success (as we saw in Chapter 4), but social media measurements such as the number of likes and shares are only part of the picture. Such vanity metrics tell you very little about what's actually going on. They are not indicators of success.

In texts such as *Social Media ROI: Managing and Measuring Social Media Efforts in Your Organisation* by Oliver Blanchard and *Social Media Metrics: How to Measure and Optimise Your Marketing*

*Investment* by Jim Stearne, you can find lists of everything you can measure for social media. All agree that these lists are thing you *could* look at, but it makes much more sense to list the measurements that are relevant to you and your business, and focus on them.

In Chapter 2, we realised that social media is not a strategy, but a detail of the business plan. Therefore it makes sense that our primary measurement is against those business objectives. The examples we used to illustrate this point were:

Strategy:   To acquire new customers, and to ensure repeat purchases by existing customers
Objective: To increase sales of a certain product by x% by a certain date
Tactic:      To publish special offers on Twitter

Strategy:   To identify, develop and recruit new donors, in the age group 18–25
Objective: To raise £x for a certain cause by a certain date
Tactic:      To run a targeted advertising campaign on Facebook

And so, the measurements we need to look for as a result of social media activity are clear:

- Did sales of the targeted product increase by x% by the date you had planned?
- Did we raise £x for a certain cause by the intended date?

For each tactic you should have a detailed implementation plan, with further objectives. For example:

- to reach x people with a discount offer code (valid for three months), and achieve a x% redemption rate
- to drive x number of visitors to a website landing page over a week, with the aim of x% providing their email address details.

While it is important to measure and review the results of your social media activity, this should not take hours; if time has been well spent in the planning stages then the measurements you need to review can be collated into a format that you can use to review and refine your activity. Your reporting format will be unique to you and your business. You may also wish to report on key competitor activity. Remember, you only need to measure what matters, and what is meaningful.

## Three key measures of success

There are three key measures of success that interact to create the social media big picture: *volume*, *engagement* and *traffic*. Let's look at these briefly before reviewing where to find the information.

|  | LinkedIn | Twitter | Facebook | Instagram | Google+ |
|---|---|---|---|---|---|
| **Volume: Audience** | Connections<br><br>Followers | Followers | Page likes | Followers | Have you in circles |
| **Volume: Amplification** | Likes<br><br>Comments<br><br>Shares | Retweets<br><br>Mentions | Shares | Likes | Shares<br><br>Mentions |
| **Engagement** | Likes<br><br>Comments<br><br>Shares | Retweets<br><br>Mentions | Shares | Likes | Shares<br><br>Mentions |
| **Engagement: Applause** | Likes | Likes | Likes | Likes | +1s |
| **Traffic** | Visits | Visits | Visits | Visits | Visits |

*Figure 7.1. Social media measures of success.*

## Volume

*Volume* metrics such as reach and amplification can be used to measure *awareness* – they can be used to see how far your message is spreading. Here we could look at follower growth rate, percentage change over time in followers, and audience demographics (to ensure the volume is in the right places). Note: people who like a Facebook page are usually referred to as fans.

## *Reach*

Reach refers to the total number of followers/fans/connections that have a chance to see your posts at any given point in time (see Figure 7.2). Note, this is different to the total number of followers/fans/connections you might have. The higher your reach, the higher your chance to engage with your audience. Reach is a great volume metric, but it does not give an indication of quality or impact/effectiveness. As we discussed in Chapter 6, the time of day/day of the week you post a message can really have an influence: look for the times when your reach is highest, and post future messages during those times.

## *Amplification*

Amplification is the rate at which your followers/fans/connections take your content and share it through their network with a like, comment, Retweet, share or mention. This can happen at any time – I often find new followers share and like older content, whereas existing followers share almost immediately. Like follower growth, amplification rate is a good benchmark metric to monitor your progress.

## Engagement

In Chapter 6 we noted the importance of engagement as a way to move potential customers through the buying decision process. We also highlighted the primary goal of content to be about starting a conversation.

If you want to measure *engagement*, take another look at the metrics around likes, shares, Retweets, mentions, comments and replies.

How many people are sharing your messages, and how often? How much do they like your content (*applause*)? What type of content do they share the most? Take a look at what content gets shared and adjust your plan to repost, or produce, more content of that type. Who is sharing? How influential are they? Use the aforementioned tools, Klout and Kred, to assess who is engaging. Are they part of your target audience?

**Reach =**

$$\frac{\text{number of fans who saw a particular post}}{\text{number of fans online at the time}}$$

**Amplification rate =**

$$\frac{\text{number of retweets or shares}}{\text{posts}}$$

**Applause rate =**

number of favourites or likes per post.

**Engagement rate =**

$$\frac{\text{sum of interactions across a social media platform}}{\substack{\text{total number of fans/followers/connections} \\ \text{on that social media platform.}}}$$

*Figure 7.2. Calculations for measuring volume and social media engagement*

Volume and engagement metrics are useful indicators of interaction, and for competitor benchmarking. But what happens next, and what more can we measure?

## Traffic

If your goal is to drive traffic to your website, then track URL shares, clicks and conversions. Also, take a look at what people are doing once they're on your website. Are you capturing leads generated and monitoring how they convert into prospects and customers?

Sources of website traffic (referrals) can provide a good indication of how people interact with social media content. Add to that a bounce-rate figure, that is the percentage of visitors to your website who navigate away from the site after viewing only one page, and you can compare social media generated traffic to other sources of web traffic.

*Conversion* is measured by providing an answer to a very simple question: What action do you want people to take once they've engaged with your content? If you want them to fill in a form, that's a conversion. If you want them to purchase something, the sale is a conversion.

However, it is important to realise that this click-through from social media platform to website may be impacted by other causes and effects over the long term. Undoubtedly, there would be additional tactics to those mentioned in these examples; it is very rare to employ only one marketing tactic within a marketing plan, which is another issue contributing to the difficulty of measuring social media.

So, how far can we go in measuring the performance of our example tactic 'to publish special offers on Twitter' or 'to run a targeted advertising campaign on Facebook' towards achieving those objectives?

Well, it depends on the specifics of the tactics we employed, and whether we made them measurable. We need to set goals based on actions that convert into something tangible (such as a captured email address). If that email address is from someone who matches the criteria of your target audience, then you can count that as a qualified lead.

For example, did the Tweet or Facebook campaign include a click-through to a specific website page? What information was included on that website page? Did you try to make a product sale or ask for a donation straight away? It's more likely that there are a number of points along the journey from a first website visit to the final conversion – perhaps providing a downloadable brochure about the product, which triggered a follow-up email and telephone call before making the sale/ receiving the donation.

Whatever you do, make sure you know what you want to measure before you start using social media; it's not a bolt-on activity. As Galileo Galilei said 'measure what can be measured and and make measurable what cannot be measured.'

• • •

These measurements can all be identified using native analytics, third-party measurement tools and website analytics. You will find links to resources concerning third-party measurement tools and website analytics in the resource section of this book. There are so many available that my advice is to consider first what you need to measure, then find the most appropriate tool/s. It's very easy to get distracted by metrics and data you might not need, even though it's nice to have.

## Native analytics

Many social media platforms, including LinkedIn, Twitter and Facebook, come with native analytic tools that will show information about your audience and content performance. They should be your first stop.

On **LinkedIn**, for personal profiles you can view data about who's viewed your profile, who's viewed your posts, and how you rank for profile views. Some data access is restricted if you have a free account. Take a look: not only is it useful performance data, but it can tell you if you're reaching the right audience profiles and give you some ideas for how you might improve your profile to rank higher among your connections, colleagues and peers. Company page analytics provide reach and engagement metrics for each post, as well as follower demographics and trends.

On **Twitter** you will find a small graph icon below each Tweet. This will show you how many impressions and engagements each post has made. Twitter Analytics provides a whole range of detailed information including Tweet highlights – Top Tweet, Top mention, Top follower, Top media Tweet) as well as Tweet impressions, profile visits, mentions and follower growth. Audience insight is also available, including the interests, gender, location, and household income categories of your audience, and more.

**Facebook** pages will display a 'people reached' figure below each post to show how many users have seen the update. The Insights tab gives a broader overview of your page performance, including views, likes, actions, reach and engagements. Here you will also find demographic information for the people who like your page, the people you reached and the people who engaged.

If social media platforms do not include native analytics, such as Instagram and Google+, other measurement tools are available. I use **Hootsuite** as my social media management tool for scheduling posts, and also use its reporting tools. Hootsuite supports LinkedIn, Twitter, Facebook, Instagram and Google+ pages (and many more).

For a more detailed guide to native analytics, please visit my website, luanwise.co.uk.

## How to calculate social media return on investment (ROI)

This chapter is all about proving the value of social media to your organisation's overall goals and business objectives, and it therefore wouldn't be complete without an ROI calculation.

Although many people see social media as a low-cost activity, there are in fact a number of costs involved, including:

- internal resources, e.g. management time
- external resources, e.g. graphic design
- social media management tools, e.g. Hootsuite
- advertising costs – if you're sponsoring content on LinkedIn, running a promoted Tweet, or boosting a Facebook post, don't forget to include the cost.

$$\text{Social media ROI} = \frac{\text{revenue from social media} - \text{cost of social media activity}}{\text{cost of social media activity.}}$$

Figure 7.3. How to calculate social media ROI.

At its simplest, a social media ROI calculation (Figure 7.3) could be completed using Google Analytics and sales data. For example:

- 1,000 clicks from ten social media campaign posts on Twitter.
- Of those 1,000 clicks, 500 converted to a lead, by filling in a form on a landing page.
- Of those 500 leads, 100 of those leads ended up making a purchase.
- This means our traffic-to-lead conversion ratio is 50%, and our lead-to-sale conversion ratio is 20%.

- We know each purchase generates £100 of revenue, and £500 of resources was allocated to the ten campaign posts.
- The campaign generated £10,000 of revenue.
- The ROI is 19:1 (for every £1 spent, £19 of profit was generated).

## Rinse and repeat

The point of tracking your social media ROI isn't just to prove your social media activity has a value, but to use the results to continually improve your activity and increase that value.

It's OK to have less than stellar results occasionally, especially when you're just starting out. The key is to have a plan of action for how you'll improve the results moving forward.

You might wish to have ongoing, overarching top-level metrics as well as campaign-focused metrics for activities that might have a clearer beginning and end, such as seasonal promotions or competitions.

Recording of metrics should be ongoing and reviewed at regular intervals, perhaps monthly. Review too infrequently and the information can build up and become too much to process, or you might miss opportunities to optimise. Review too often and you could invest a lot of effort without gaining any further benefit, or be tempted to act without having built up a true understanding.

For example, if you are driving traffic to your website via social media, but have a low conversion rate, it could be that your content attracts the wrong people or there is a confusing user experience on your landing page. Testing is widely used in marketing, so try something different – making just one change at a time – and measure the results. Rinse, and repeat.

# Relax!

- There is no 'one size fits all' approach to measuring social media. You will need to select the appropriate data and tools to match your business objectives.
- Social media measurement has two roles – to evaluate activity and to help optimise activity.
- Take a look at the native analytics for each of the social media platforms you are using.
- Include competitor benchmarking to your reports, if required.
- Review your results regularly and identify areas in which you could make improvements. If you know what you need to do when you see the metric, it's meaningful (and therefore matters).

# CHAPTER 8
## Making it happen

© Clarketoons.com

Individuals and businesses that are successful with social media don't fall into the 'social media's the answer; what's the question?' trap. They define what they are trying to achieve, and the best way to achieve it, then find the tools they need to achieve their goals.

> Some people want it to happen, some wish
> it could happen, others make it happen.
> MICHAEL JORDAN

In this final chapter we look at 'making it happen'. I hope you have followed the planning journey through this book and are now feeling more relaxed. Your fears have been quelled, and you're ready to take the next steps to success.

Here's a summary of what we've learnt so far:

- Start with *why*. Set your strategy and SMART objectives.
- Size doesn't matter, and you can't do it all – the size of a social media platform may inspire us to act, but doesn't show us how to act, or tell us whether it's the right place to be.
- Your social media plan will be guided by your audience – define their persona, understand their needs, wants and the information they need along the buyer journey.
- Select the platform where you can find your target audience.
- Be ready to do business – complete all sections of your profile, add a great photo, and optimise your headline/bio/about sections.
- Be ready to reply to people – set up a plan for listening, and think about how you might respond to complaints, compliments and other issues.
- Stay active: be in front of your audience at the right time, with shareable content.
- Focus on building relationships, and engaging in conversation.
- Keep it simple. Measure activity against your objectives and look closely at the metrics that matter most.

## Social media management tools

So, making it happen. It might take some time (days) to prepare your plan and update your profiles. Once a month, you might spend time reviewing your results and updating your plan. Content creation and curation take as much time as you have available and, unless you're running high-volume social customer service activity, ten minutes a day is all you need to stay on top of this communication channel.

• • •

First, for each of the platforms you are using, go to 'settings' and switch on notifications so you receive alerts via email or to mobile devices. Receiving alerts to important information is really helpful. Decide what you need to be made aware of – and change your settings if/when specific circumstances arise. For example if you have a potential crisis or a timely campaign is running.

Second, use social media management tools to save time. I use **Hootsuite** as it provides a single dashboard to manage multiple social media profiles, and I can schedule content, track keywords (hashtags), mentions and view results. Hootsuite offers free, pro and enterprise packages. It's also really useful if you have a team of people managing social media activity.

Other similar tools include **Tweetdeck**, which is now only for Twitter monitoring, and **Buffer**. Buffer has superior scheduling flexibility. Some people use Hootsuite to listen and Buffer to schedule. **MeetEdgar** is another scheduling application, perfect if you have lots of evergreen content, as it allows you to group content into specific categories for sharing across multiple platforms.

My advice is to define what you need, and then go looking for the solution. Ask for recommendations and do a free trial to see if it works for you. There are many other social media management tools, and a directory listing is included in the resource section.

Others I use include **Tweriod**, a free Twitter tool that helps you find out when your Twitter followers are online the most; **Crowdfire,** which helps manage Twitter and Instagram account following/followers; plus **Google**

**Alerts**, **Twilert** and **Followerwonk**, which were mentioned in Chapter 5. I also use **Feedly** for content curation, as mentioned in Chapter 6.

## Managing risk

Finally, despite all the positive vibes about social media throughout this book, it is important to note that there are also risks involved. Social media is not a task confined to marketing teams, and it is not confined to the workplace from 9 to 5.

All users of social media should review the 'terms of use' for the social media platforms they use, to ensure compliance.

Sadly, there have been cases of employees criticising their colleagues or employers online, leaking confidential information and/or undermining their own professional credibility by sharing personal views that are not compatible with their professional role.

Problems that can occur online include defamation, discrimination, obscenity, harassment, data protection issues, trade descriptions issues, IP rights, brand reputation and the confidentiality of sensitive business information. These issues are not unique to social media.

Legally, conversations on social media are no different to any other conversation. As yet, there is no specific legislation related to social media use. There is, however, a clear need to create guidelines, provide training and send out regular internal communications to all employees in an organisation, to remind them what is appropriate online behaviour – and what is not.

A social media policy should provide guidelines for employees representing an organisation on social media, and also for those using personal profiles in a way that might affect the business. A social media policy might be part of an internet use policy, and should reference other policies such as equal opportunities and anti-harassment.

However, due to the real-time nature of social media, it is too restrictive to fully script all social media activity. This is not a website or printed brochure that takes several weeks to prepare and needs the input of many individuals. Staff need to know exactly what their social media roles and responsibilities are, and be empowered to make their own choices about how to act or respond.

Where should you start? By taking a common-sense approach, focusing on the positives, and reminding employees of possible consequences.

Everyone in an organisation, no matter its size, needs to understand what information counts as personal information and how to avoid using it in a public space (no matter what your privacy settings, some information is still publicly available).

A social media policy should make clear what is confidential information and set out what it regards as acceptable behaviour – and what is unacceptable. Particularly, customers or contacts should not be mentioned without getting their explicit permission in advance.

Guidelines are also likely to be set around:

- target response times to queries
- working hours/out-of-hours activity
- negative comments about company or staff
- comments that might be considered offensive (on race, gender, religion, etc.)
- handling and reporting inappropriate content
- recording and reporting information
- how/where to obtain further information or advice
- the consequences of breaching social media policy and how the disciplinary process will operate.

It is a good idea to get a lawyer to check your social media policy to ensure your business is adequately protected from liability. All staff should be asked to read the policy (and sign a document to that end) when it is introduced;

it should also be part of the induction process for new staff. A link to examples of social media policies is included in the resources section.

## How to nail social media in ten minutes a day

One of the questions I am asked most frequently during social media talks is: 'How do you find the time to do all this?'

My initial answer is, I'm not an 'average' social media user. I manage multiple accounts and ensure I stay up to date in order to provide the most effective training courses. My daily routine involves switching off my alarm and checking my smartphone. I then check Facebook, Twitter, LinkedIn and increasingly Instagram. I 'like' a few things, often as a way to remind me to read them later on. I 'check in' during the day — depending on where I am and what I'm doing — usually mid-morning and just after lunch, as my newsfeeds contain the most new content at these times. I'll look at Google+ a couple of times a week. Using my smartphone is fine for this, but to do 'real' work, I always use the desktop.

But if I was an 'average' social media user, what would I recommend? Up to an hour a week, plus ten minutes a day: this is all you need to maintain an effective presence and get results.

My 'evergreen' content -that is, content which does not expire in the short term - and 'what I'm doing' content is pre-scheduled using Feedly and Hootsuite. This takes me about 30 minutes. In ten minutes a day I have time to check my notifications and newsfeed/timeline, share new content, and engage with connections or followers — it doesn't take long to say a quick 'thank you' or click the 'like' button. Once or twice a week you should check who has viewed your profile on LinkedIn, and participate in a group discussion. I also schedule additional time to manage LinkedIn invitations and build my audiences: another 15 minutes a week, perhaps.

Regular participation will ensure you soon have a manageable way of acquiring news and information, and of engaging in meaningful conversations. We all spend much longer than this tackling our email inbox each day, don't we? Technology is here to make our lives easier. It's not fundamentally changing what we do — just how we do it.

## Don't let social media replace face-to-face conversation

I posted the article below on my LinkedIn profile in August 2014. In training sessions I share lots of case studies to show that it's possible for anyone to achieve success with social media if they have defined their key messages, know their audience, have a plan, and work it hard. The 'how to' of using individual social media platforms is relatively easy to understand in comparison.

It took about an hour to write, in my home office, in my pyjamas. It didn't cost anything, and it has produced measurable benefits. On the day I first posted it, in addition to comments and shares, I received complimentary Tweets, followed by a telephone enquiry asking if I could close a conference with a talk on the same subject. Of course I could! That conference achieved significant reach on Twitter. So far I've been invited back to speak at another three conferences for the same organiser. The article has now been viewed over 10,000 times and makes regular appearances on Twitter (it's truly evergreen). I hope you like it too.

*Before the internet we wrote letters, made phone calls and met people face to face.*

*Things move on, and at a rapid pace.*

*Don't get me wrong; I love online social networking. I can spend hours ensuring sites such as Twitter and LinkedIn are working hard for my business (and on behalf of my clients' businesses). I also spend hours reading and talking about social media. Social media takes time, but it saves time too. It's flexible, accessible 24/7, and crosses geographical boundaries.*

*Yet it's all too easy to get the balance wrong. Online can take over and become a comfort blanket to the real world. Conversations become functional correspondence, and personalities can get lost.*

*So, what is the answer?*

*Face-to-face is still the most important method of communication. There are no 140-character limits, and no hiding behind a screen. Body language and tone of voice are in play.*

*Nothing beats a good chat over a cup of coffee. This is where the most important conversations take place – where you discover your clients' biggest concerns, and see how you can help.*

*Online interactions should never replace offline interactions – one should support the other.*

*My first realisation that there was an audience behind the content I was posting online came at an industry exhibition. An existing contact introduced me to a colleague who said, 'I've seen you on LinkedIn. You're very active in groups.'*

*Eek. And yay – this stuff works. Up to that point I hadn't given much thought to life beyond my screen. I'd got caught up in the technology and had forgotten the audience.*

*I now use social media tools to find new people to meet. I use search criteria to research people and, if relevant, make initial contact. I then ask if we can meet for coffee, because face-to-face meetings are when the real connections are made.*

*It might be that I've found we have something in common – we're both attending the same industry event, for example: the perfect place to meet up.*

*If I meet new people at an event, the first thing I do when I return to my desk is continue the conversation. I'll follow them on Twitter and connect on LinkedIn. Most importantly, I'll personalise my connection request with information about how we met – or refer to something we discussed. I can then nurture the relationship through social media until the next time we speak or meet.*

*So, don't let social media replace the personal touch – use it to enhance your business relationships and you'll soon see the results.*

## Relax!

- Use social media management tools to save time. Define what you need and seek recommendations for a solution that will work best for you and your business.
- Create guidelines, provide training and regular internal communications for colleagues and associates representing your business.
- Plan your time and create a habit for using social media. Integrate your online and offline worlds. Ask your social media connections, followers, fans to meet up in real-life.

# Resources

© Clarketoons.com

Throughout this book I have referred to a number of websites, books, papers and social media tools, and I have listed them below. I hope you find them helpful.

## Social media platforms

**LinkedIn updates:**
business.linkedin.com/en-uk/marketing-solutions/blog
**Twitter updates:**
blog.twitter.com
**Facebook updates:**
newsroom.fb.com/news
**Instagram updates:**
instagram.com/press
**Google+ updates:**
googleblog.blogspot.co.uk

• • •

## Useful social media tools and further information

**Brandwatch** – brandwatch.com
**Buffer** – buffer.com
**Crowdfire** – crowdfireapp.com
**Feedly** – feedly.com
**Followerwonk** – followerwonk.com
**Google Alerts** – google.co.uk/alerts
**Google Analytics** – analytics.google.com
**Hashtags.org** – hashtags.org
**Hashtagify** – hashtagify.me
**Hootsuite** – hootsuite.com
**If This Then That** – ifttt.com
**Klout** – klout.com
**Kred** – kred.com
**MeetEdgar** – meetedgar.com
**MeltwaterBuzz** – meltwater.com
**Radian6** - marketingcloud.com/products/social-media-marketing/radian6
**Slideshare** – slideshare.net
**Tweetdeck** – Tweetdeck.twitter.com
**Tweriod** – tweriod.com

**Twilert** – twilert.com
**Twitter Advanced Search** – twitter.com/search-advanced
**Twitter Analytics** – analytics.twitter.com

**Social media listening tools comparison:**
smartinsights.com/social-media-marketing/social-media-analytics/
social-media-listening-tool-comparison/

**Social media policies:**
socialmediagovernance.com/policies

**Social media tools directory:**
Socdir.com

• • •

**Social media case studies**

**Direct Marketing Association awards:**
dma.org.uk/awards

**The Drum Social Buzz awards:**
socialbuzzawards.com

• • •

**Market research resources**

**eMarketer** – emarketer.com
**Keynote** – keynote.co.uk
**Mintel** – mintel.com
**Nielson** – nielson.com
**YouGov** – yougov.co.uk

• • •

# REFERENCES

Aimia (2012) 'Staring at the Sun: Identifying, Understanding and Influencing Social Media.' Available at: aimia.com/content/dam/aimiawebsite/CaseStudiesWhitepapersResearch/english/Aimia_SocialMedia_Whitepaper.pdf

Pete Blackshaw (2008) *Satisfied Customers Tell Three Friends, Angry Customers Tell 3,000: Running a Business in Today's Consumer-Driven World*. Doubleday.

Olivier Blanchard (2011) *Social Media ROI: Managing and Measuring Social Media Efforts in Your Organization*. Que

Stephen R. Covey (1989/2004) *The 7 Habits of Highly Effective People*. Simon & Schuster.

Robin Dunbar (2010) *How Many Friends Does One Person Need?: Dunbar's Number and Other Evolutionary Quirks*. Faber & Faber.

Andy Headworth (2015) *Social Media Recruitment: How to Successfully Integrate Social Media into Recruitment Strategy*. Kogan Page.

Chip Heath and Dan Heath (2008) *Made to Stick*. Arrow.

Sonja Jefferson and Sharon Tanton (First Edition, 2013) *Valuable Content Marketing*. Kogan Page.

Jan H. Kietzmann, Kristopher Hermkens, Ian P. McCarthy and Bruno S. Silvestre (2011) 'Social media? Get serious! Understanding the functional building blocks of social media.' *Business Horizons*, 54(3): 241–251.

Jim Stearne (2010) *Social Media Metrics: How to Measure and Optimize Your Marketing Investment*. Wiley.

Will Kintish (2014) *Business Networking – The Survival Guide: How to Make Networking Less about Stress and More about Success.* Pearson.

Mark Prensky (2001) 'Digital natives, digital immigrants'. Available at: marcprensky.com/writing/Prensky%20-%20Digital%20Natives,%20 Digital%20Immigrants%20-%20Part1.pdf

Stephen D. Rappaport (2011) *Listen First! Turning Social Media Conversations into Business Advantage.* Wiley.

Al Ries and Jack Trout (2001) *Positioning: The Battle for your Mind.* McGraw-Hill.

Simon Sinek (2009) *Start with Why: How Great Leaders Inspire Everyone to Take Action.* Penguin.

• • •

For other free resources, visit luanwise.co.uk/how-i-help. There you will find a range of downloads on various topics, including:

- how to do keyword research
- how to set up a Facebook page for your business
- how to set up Google Analytics
- how using Google Analytics can improve your website performance and social campaigns
- how to improve your search rankings with a Google+ page
- a LinkedIn Advanced Search checklist
- my LinkedIn top tips
- how to set up an Instagram page for your business
- a social media messaging plan template and worked examples
- no-nonsense social media glossary
- my top marketing resources.

**E-learning**

I have developed a number of e-learning courses that provide up-to-date 'how to' learning for LinkedIn and Twitter.

Readers of this book can benefit from a 25% discount on all e-learning courses. Just enter 'coffee' as the promo code at checkout. To get started, visit luanwise.co.uk/how-i-help/e-learning.

Courses available include:

- Getting started with LinkedIn
- Building your LinkedIn network
- How to search LinkedIn
- LinkedIn groups
- LinkedIn company pages
- Twitter essentials.

• • •

**Connect with me:**

**luanwise.co.uk**
**twitter.com/luanwise**
**linkedin.com/in/luanwise**
**plus.google.com/+luanwiseltd**
**instagram.com/luanwise**
**facebook.com/luanwise**
**slideshare.net/luanwise**

# Acknowledgements

> She believed she could, so she did.
>
> R.S. GREY

Wow. Finally, it's the end – or is it just another beginning? Writing a book was on my list of things to do before I was 40 (tick). When I started the process I had an idea of what I wanted to achieve, but it wasn't until I actually started writing that the title and the story became clear (it's ironic that most of the book is about planning, I know).

At the start of 2016 I spoke at a breakfast networking event and met Kim Fleet, a published author, who stood up and spoke about how she helped writers overcome procrastination. After one coffee meeting with Kim, I was ready to go. I was committed. Thank you, Kim, for keeping me on track, for the cups of coffee, and for your wonderful advice to reward milestones with treats!

Thank you to Nigel, who first convinced me to take a look at social media. You were right! Thank you to my friends for listening to me talk about not much else apart from the book for six months. Fiona, Flick, and Jo thank you. Additional thanks go to Penny for offering 'what's the point?' as the subject talk title that set me on this path! Thank you to Lawrence for all the debate about metrics; Neil for graphic design; Phil for illustrations; Jen for the photography; and to Jane Hammett for copy-editing the book. Thanks also to those who reviewed content and provided feedback.

To my clients and those who have attended my talks, thank you for clarifying my thinking and listening to what I have to say. To Kelly, my first (and best) boss, for helping me on my way to becoming the marketer and the person I am today. Nick and Graham, if you're reading this, you were great bosses too! To Nicola, for being the one to help me spend my hard-earned cash – you're the best shopping companion ever. To my brother Neil and his growing family, and to Mum for your never-ending support. Dad, I'm sorry you're not here to see this. I miss you.

Finally to Steve, my husband and best friend. Thank you for your patience and for everything you do. And Taylor – maybe, just maybe, you might write a review of this in your homework diary? ☺